WORLD PHILOSOPHY SERIES

THE UNHOLY ALLIANCE OF SCIENCE AND ANALYTIC EPISTEMOLOGY

ON THE TURN TO VIRTUE IN CONTEMPORARY ANALYTIC PHILOSOPHY

WORLD PHILOSOPHY SERIES

Additional books in this series can be found on Nova's website
under the Series tab.

Additional E-books in this series can be found on Nova's website
under the E-book tab.

WORLD PHILOSOPHY SERIES

THE UNHOLY ALLIANCE OF SCIENCE AND ANALYTIC EPISTEMOLOGY

ON THE TURN TO VIRTUE IN CONTEMPORARY ANALYTIC PHILOSOPHY

DANIEL P. HAGGERTY

Nova Science Publishers, Inc.
New York

Copyright © 2011 by Nova Science Publishers, Inc.

All rights reserved. No part of this book may be reproduced, stored in a retrieval system or transmitted in any form or by any means: electronic, electrostatic, magnetic, tape, mechanical photocopying, recording or otherwise without the written permission of the Publisher.

For permission to use material from this book please contact us:
Telephone 631-231-7269; Fax 631-231-8175
Web Site: http://www.novapublishers.com

NOTICE TO THE READER

The Publisher has taken reasonable care in the preparation of this book, but makes no expressed or implied warranty of any kind and assumes no responsibility for any errors or omissions. No liability is assumed for incidental or consequential damages in connection with or arising out of information contained in this book. The Publisher shall not be liable for any special, consequential, or exemplary damages resulting, in whole or in part, from the readers' use of, or reliance upon, this material. Any parts of this book based on government reports are so indicated and copyright is claimed for those parts to the extent applicable to compilations of such works.

Independent verification should be sought for any data, advice or recommendations contained in this book. In addition, no responsibility is assumed by the publisher for any injury and/or damage to persons or property arising from any methods, products, instructions, ideas or otherwise contained in this publication.

This publication is designed to provide accurate and authoritative information with regard to the subject matter covered herein. It is sold with the clear understanding that the Publisher is not engaged in rendering legal or any other professional services. If legal or any other expert assistance is required, the services of a competent person should be sought. FROM A DECLARATION OF PARTICIPANTS JOINTLY ADOPTED BY A COMMITTEE OF THE AMERICAN BAR ASSOCIATION AND A COMMITTEE OF PUBLISHERS.

Additional color graphics may be available in the e-book version of this book.

Library of Congress Cataloging-in-Publication Data

Haggerty, Daniel P.
  The unholy alliance of science and analytic epistemology : on the turn to virtue in contemporary analytic philosophy / Daniel P. Haggerty.
      p. cm.
  Includes bibliographical references and index.
  ISBN 978-1-61324-873-7 (softcover)
  1. Science--Philosophy. 2. Virtue epistemology. I. Title.
  Q175.32.V57H34 2011
  121--dc23
                                                                            2011017615

Published by Nova Science Publishers, Inc. † New York

For my family

CONTENTS

Preface		ix
Introduction		1
Chapter 1	Return to Virtue	5
Chapter 2	Virtue Ethics	17
Chapter 3	From Hume to Quine: The Separation of Ethics and Epistemology and the Rise of Analytic Philosophy	37
Chapter 4	Virtue Epistemology: From (JTB) to (VE)	61
Chapter 5	Epistemology and Ethics	79
References		93
Index		99

PREFACE

This book is part intellectual geography, part argumentative essay. It is written for members of the scientific community broadly construed. It may appeal to such a community insofar as it shows that contemporary analytic epistemology and virtue ethics have their roots in the modern scientific method. Students and specialists in epistemology might also find the book useful as it provides an historical and conceptual orientation to help the reader understand the broader context in which the technical work that goes on inside contemporary analytic epistemology takes place.

As a work in intellectual geography, the book shows the profound influence of modern scientific method on twentieth century analytic epistemology. Anglo-American philosophers so captivated by the power of modern science and concomitant advances in logic and mathematics took—or rather, mistook—all knowledge to be reducible to the propositions of science and logic. Ethics, along with metaphysics and religion, were cast off as mere expressions of sentiment at best, or as utter nonsense at worst. In order to reveal this most remarkable situation I track developments in intellectual culture from Kepler, Newton, and Hume to Frege, Husserl, Hempel and Quine; developments which led to the rise and fall of logical empiricism—the view that all knowledge is based on logical inference from observation statements. I also track the parallel rise and fall of modern moral philosophy, the attempt to model moral theory on logic and empiricism.

I show how the recent rediscovery and redeployment of the ancient philosophical concept 'virtue' resuscitated first ethics and then epistemology. Though many contemporary theorists of virtue ethics seem to ignore or only glance at Aristotle's work on the subject, while still others reject it outright, I contend that we cannot grasp the meaning of 'virtue ethics' adequately without a reasonably firm hold of Aristotle's work on the subject. For this reason I trace the heart of contemporary virtue ethics by reference to Aristotle, whose contributions to the field remain unsurpassed. I then go on to sketch the development of contemporary virtue epistemology out of various considerations involving analyses of the concept 'epistemic justification'. Emerging divisions between virtue-reliabilism and virtue-responsibilism in epistemology are also presented.

In addition to the intellectual geography provided, the book also advances a line of argument that pairs elements of the work of John McDowell with insights from Aristotle. I contend that contrary to a three-hundred year tradition of thought that runs from Hume to Hempel and on, scientific and ethical reasoning are not logically distinct. It is not the case, I argue, that scientific explanation deals with "matters of fact" which are disconnected logically from normative claims—that is, claims about value, about what is good, desirable and so forth. I draw substantially from the work of McDowell on the relation of mind and world to show how scientific and ethical knowledge involve the same kind of intelligibility, namely, one that is essentially normative. They both occupy the logical space of reasons, the domain of epistemology where concepts of 'evidence', 'justification', and 'explanation' get instantiated.

By contrast the logical space of nature, according to McDowell, is the realm of *law*. It is not the realm of reasons, justifications and explanations, whether natural scientific or ethical. Forays in the logical space of nature aim at a mode of understanding that is different in kind from normative epistemology. Such understanding is conceptualized in terms of Aristotle's account of *theoria* and the intellectual virtues and aims it encompasses. *Theoria* involves a kind of intelligibility common to pure science and metaphysics. To be sure such understanding has a certain value. Indeed if Aristotle is to be trusted it is a kind of intelligibility that constitutes ultimate happiness. Such value, however, outstrips the normativity of ethics and epistemology in the logical space of reasons.

INTRODUCTION

By the 18th century, European philosophers and scientists began to distinguish sharply between descriptive explanations and prescriptive evaluations. The former were conceived of in terms of the natural, the latter in terms of the normative. The consequences of this distinction were considerable. Modern science stood on the side of the descriptive and the explanatory—the presumed field of knowledge. Metaphysics, ethics and religion stood on the other side—the field of value. To this day efforts are made to reconcile or reintegrate science and religion, or science and ethics. In this book I wish to show some of the most important ways in which epistemology (including scientific knowledge) and ethics are being rejoined in contemporary philosophy around the ancient philosophical concept 'virtue'.

The focus of this book is the development of virtue ethics and virtue epistemology in recent analytic philosophy. The aim is to provide members of the scientific community and other non-specialists with an overview of these developments, and what they mean for the current state of knowledge and value. More particularly, the book aims to show the end of a putative dichotomy between the natural and the normative, between facts and values, and the implications for ethics and epistemology in contemporary English speaking philosophy.

Chapter one begins with important distinctions and definitions of key terms. It moves on to explain the reasons for the revival of virtue ethics in twentieth century analytic philosophy. In short, the return to virtue ethics develops out of philosophical dissatisfaction with modern ethical theories— particularly utilitarianism and Kant's deontology. The problem with modern moral theories is that they attempt to make sense of the notion of moral law without a tenable notion of a lawgiver. Absent a theological or religious framework for moral philosophy, a return to the ancient concept of ethical virtue is most promising.

Chapter two presents a more thoroughgoing account of virtue ethics. I draw heavily from the work of Aristotle who remains unsurpassed on the nature of virtue. The distinction between the ancient notion of *ēthikē aretē* (virtue ethics) and the contemporary meaning of "moral virtue" is drawn. The meaning of the latter is shown to have developed out of Roman and Latin renderings of ancient Greek concepts, ultimately wrought in English. The sense in which character virtues are active conditions of the soul, according to Aristotle, is explained. Finally, a few particular virtues and their corresponding vices are analyzed.

Chapter three explores the separation of ethics and epistemology in modern philosophy, the same era in which modern moral theories were developed. The separation between ethics and epistemology, or between knowledge and morality, is attributed first to the work of David Hume. Hume's arguments are then set against the background of the concomitant rise of the modern scientific method, which reinforced the idea of a dichotomy between the natural and the normative. Modern scientific method also rejected teleology, a mode of putative "natural explanation" dating back to Aristotle and continuing through medieval philosophy. Rejection of teleology meant the denunciation of natural law theories of ethics and the genesis of modern moral theories. Finally, the culmination of the separation of ethics and epistemology in early analytic philosophy is explained in terms of developments in the philosophy of mathematics at the beginning of the twentieth century. Implications for epistemology are explored.

Chapter four charts the development of analytic epistemology in the second half of the twentieth century. Conceptual analysis of 'knowledge' led to a close and protracted scrutiny of the notion of 'epistemic justification'. This in turn gave rise to competing theories of the structure of epistemic justification. Meanwhile, Quine's arguments for rejecting epistemology in favor of cognitive science led epistemologists to make explicit the normative, and thus non-reductive, nature of knowledge. Emphasis on the normativity of knowledge generally and epistemic justification in particular is followed by the notion of epistemic desiderata—the idea that there is no one unified concept of epistemic justification, but plural epistemic values. Finally, together with analysis of 'epistemic justification' dissatisfaction with competing theories of the structure of justification resulted in new interest in the notion of intellectual virtues, and the birth of contemporary virtue epistemology.

In chapter five I argue that ethics and epistemology belong to the same logical space of reasons, and that they share the same ultimate aims. As such, they are by nature inseparable. I contend that ethics and epistemology share a common source of normativity insofar as both are concerned with reasons and answerability to the world. The logical space of nature, on the other hand, is the domain of "pure" science and metaphysics. This is a mode of intelligibility that involves observation, description and mathematical precision independent of reasons and causal explanations. As such, it is not the locus of natural scientific explanation—instead all such explanations belong to the logical space as epistemology and ethics.

Of course there is much that this book leaves out. What is included, moreover, is not treated as exhaustively as possible. In particular, the reasons for the separation of ethics and epistemology discussed in Chapter three and the overview of developments in analytic epistemology in the twentieth century discussed in Chapter four are quite abbreviated. To provide a more thorough account would, however, result in a much longer book that would fail to meet to one of the primary goals of this one, namely, to provide a wieldy narrative of developments that stand behind and support some of the most interesting work in contemporary philosophy.

Chapter 1

RETURN TO VIRTUE

PRELIMINARIES

This chapter is concerned with preliminary material. Important terms are introduced and the main reasons for reclaiming the concept 'virtue' in ethics are explained.

This book explicates the separation of ethics and epistemology in modern philosophy, that is, the period of European and eventually American philosophy beginning in the 17th century. It also accounts for present efforts to reunify the two. To begin, though, I imagine that the idea that ethics and knowledge are *not* connected may be strange to many readers. For one, it seems to be a truism that knowledge is, *ceteris paribus*, good and valuable—an important part of what makes good lives good. For another, our ordinary notions imply that morality involves knowing the difference between right and wrong. Thus some basic preliminary explanation is in order to account for the modern philosophical idea that epistemology (knowledge) is separate from ethics. A more substantive account of this view is provided in chapter three.

It is useful to begin with definitions of a few key terms. In the broadest sense, the word *ethics* refers to philosophical reflection on value. The English word "ethics" is derived from the Greek *ēthos*, which signifies the characteristic spirit or the character of a people or community. Such spirit animates what is held to be important within a given community. A military code of honor, for example, is an essential aspect of the *ēthos* characteristic of armed forces, and, ideally, of the ethical character and conduct of their members.

Etymology as well as ordinary contemporary use of the word "ethics" may make it difficult to imagine why modern philosophy separates ethics and knowledge (epistemology). Inquiry, fact finding, explanation, reasoning, criticism and revision, all of which are epistemological activities, are fundamental to the characteristic spirit of virtually every human community. In this way, matters of knowledge may seem obviously a matter of ethics—of value, of a characteristically human *ēthos*. Moreover, philosophical reflection on value includes consideration of what is valuable—and knowledge is certainly valuable. Thus philosophical ethics would seem to imply epistemology.

To understand the modern split between ethics and epistemology, then, we must narrow the scope. The recent divide between these two fields of philosophy can be understood more precisely and perspicaciously as the separation of (modern) science from *morality*. The term "morality" is defined more narrowly than ethics. Rather than reflection on the nature of value generally, "morality" refers more specifically to human actions distinguished in terms of right and wrong conduct. A code of honesty may be central to the ethics of an institution, but it is a matter of morality whether a given individual acts honestly or dishonestly.

Most generally epistemology is philosophical reflection on knowledge. Much contemporary epistemology investigates the nature and possibility of knowing, which includes the nature of belief-formation, reasoning, and explanation. In the light of this definition of epistemology, it might again seem difficult to imagine why anyone would think that knowledge has nothing to do with ethics. For we quite evidently evaluate belief-formation, reasoning and explanation as good and bad, correct and incorrect. Good and right reasoning tends to produce knowledge. Bad reasoning tends to produce false belief. Defined more narrowly, however, and in a way more suitable to present purposes, epistemology is virtually synonymous with science. Indeed, the original meaning of "science" includes the state or act of knowing—science, in this sense, is specifically knowledge acquired by study. To get to the point of separation between ethics and epistemology, however, we must understand "science" as referring even more narrowly to the modern scientific method. It is precisely this method, we have been led to believe, which can and must be free of moral evaluation.

The attitude that knowledge as scientific method must be kept apart from ethics as moral decision making comes straight out of the modern scientific revolution. It is an attitude that remains influential to this day. Of course, in one sense it is obviously correct. Scientific method is used to explain, so far as possible, how things are—the facts of the matter. It does not, or—putting aside the irony—it *ought* not to attempt to produce results that are in harmony with what anyone, or any institution, thinks should be the case. There was a time of course when science was under the control of moral and religious authority, and modern science is rightly proud of the hard fought battles to win its independence. The deeper philosophical idea at work here, however, and the claim that I dispute in this book, is that science is a purely descriptive activity, while ethics is uniquely prescriptive—this, along with the concomitant idea that the descriptive and prescriptive can and must remain apart.

Thus in the most basic terms the modern split between ethics and epistemology is the result of a distinction between descriptive explanation and prescriptive exhortation. Although we may routinely run them together in ordinary thought and language, an important legacy of modern philosophy is that the two are logically and conceptually distinct. Science produces knowledge by descriptive explanation of natural phenomena. Ethics aims to control and motivate human conduct by prescriptive exhortations. However, as I aim to show, recent work in analytic epistemology reunifies value and knowledge, reintegrating descriptive analysis and prescriptive normativity in the concept virtue.

It is important to have a working definition of "analytic philosophy" since it is from within this tradition that virtue has made a return in both ethics and epistemology. This fact is somewhat surprising, as analytic philosophy is precisely the method or style of philosophy that most closely emulates the modern scientific method itself—the method that motivated the separation of ethics and epistemology in modern philosophy in the first place. In the middle of the twentieth century, "analytic" philosophy, which is usually contrasted with "continental" philosophy, was a coherent philosophical movement in the United States and Great Britain.[1] For this reason analytic philosophy is sometimes called Anglo-American philosophy. While these terms are still very much in use today, it is certainly worth noting that, as a unified philosophical movement, analytic philosophy was undone from within by two of the most prominent figures of twentieth century American philosophy; namely, Willard Van Orman Quine (1908-2000) and Wilfred Sellars (1912-1989).

Today analytic philosophy names a *style* of doing philosophy, not a program or set of substantive views. The analytic style of philosophy mimics that of the sciences and mathematics, at least insofar as it aims for

---

[1] For more on the distinctions between analytic and continental philosophy, see Brian Leiter and Michael Rosen, T*he Oxford Handbook of Continental Philosophy* (New York: Oxford University Press, 2007).

argumentative, logical precision. The continental style, by contrast, is far more literary and identifies more closely with the humanities than the sciences. One of the most useful ways of drawing the distinction between these two contemporary philosophical styles is by pointing to how they diverge in their reactions to the philosophical work of Georg Wilhelm Friedrich Hegel (1770-1831). Continental philosophy develops out of a positive response to Hegel's rejection of philosophical analysis in favor of synthesis and speculation. Instead of separating complex ideas into their most basic constitutive elements, Hegel aims for far-reaching connections across human culture and history. Key figures in the pro-Hegelian tradition include Fichte, Schelling, Schopenhauer, Kierkegaard, Marx, Nietzsche, Husserl, Heidegger, Merleau-Ponty, Sartre, Lacan, Gadamer, Horkheimer, Adorno, Marcuse, Habermas, Foucault, Derrida, and Žižek.[2]

Analytic philosophy develops out of a negative appraisal of Hegel's philosophy; namely, that it is grandiloquent speculation unconstrained by sound principles of reasoning. Hegelian philosophy produces systematic theories of art and culture, mind and nature, God and politics, and so on. Having a disdainful response to such sweeping philosophical conjecture, analytic philosophers sought to emulate their colleagues in mathematics and the sciences by focusing on narrow topics with the utmost precision and thoroughness. The hope was that each specialist working in a narrow field of philosophy might make meaningful contributions to the collective goals of inquiry. The aim was to solve or dissolve philosophical problems—not to construct wide-ranging philosophical speculation. Key figures in the analytic tradition include Frege, Russell, Moore, Wittgenstein, Carnap, Quine, Anscombe, Strawson, Davidson, Kripke, Rawls, and Dummett. Today, certain noteworthy philosophers coming out of the analytic tradition are engaging continental themes. Robert Brandom, for example, is a distinguished analytic philosopher of language, logic, and mind who is presently engaging the work of Hegel.[3]

There is thus a certain irony that today it is philosophical work in epistemology and ethics that comes out of the analytic tradition that leads to a reunification of knowledge and value through the concept *virtue*. This approach to philosophy, which for so long eschewed synthesis in favor of analytical precision, is now the vanguard of a movement that has the potential to integrate fields of philosophy in ways characteristic of the pre-modern

---

[2] Leiter and Rosen, *The Oxford Handbook*, 1-5.
[3] *Ibid.*

scientific philosophies of antiquity. The current movement to reconcile value and knowledge grows out of the very philosophical tradition that once celebrated the divorce of epistemology from ethics, of science from morality.

THE TWENTIETH-CENTURY REVIVAL OF VIRTUE ETHICS

The recent return to virtue in Anglo-American philosophy began in ethics in the nineteen-fifties. It first reached epistemology in the nineteen-eighties. This section is concerned with the former.

From Plato (428-348 BC) and Aristotle (384-322 BC) up to the 18th century European Enlightenment, virtue ethics remained the dominant approach to philosophical ethics in the West. Put plainly, virtue ethics is concerned with the nature and development of good character. Virtues refer to traits that are constitutive of good character. By contrast, modern moral philosophy—which is to say, moral philosophy in the *modern era*, centering upon the 18th century—emphasizes the evaluation of actions, or kind of actions, rather than people and their character. Actions are evaluated in the light of their consequences (consequentialism), or in terms of whether and how well they conform to moral rules and duties (deontology).

From the perspective of early twentieth century analytic philosophy, although medieval Christian philosophers developed discussion of the virtues in the light of their conception of natural and Divine Law, the medieval addition of theological virtues did not constitute a departure from ancient virtue ethics in any theoretically interesting way. What did constitute an important departure from the virtue tradition of antiquity, again from the perspective of analytic philosophers and their peculiar appropriation of Enlightenment philosophy, was the modern era's ultimate abandonment of theological underpinnings for philosophical ethics. By the 18th century, philosophical ethics had been divorced from God and religion. This resulted in a new emphasis on acts and consequences as the proper focus of philosophical investigation in ethics. In line with the new scientific method, acts and consequences could be observed—virtues, character, and intentions could not.

Thus while Hume (1711-1776) and Kant (1724-1804), for example, did write on virtues and vices, they were seen not to treat these topics as part of the fundamental work of ethics. Instead, modern moral philosophy aimed to produce secular moral theory and investigate meta-ethical questions about what constitutes reasons for acting. By the first half of the twentieth century, Anglo-American analytic philosophers had come to regard the modern emphasis on act-evaluations as the fundamentally important philosophical legacy of Enlightenment ethics. With the rise of utilitarianism in the 19th century, philosophical discussion of the virtues and moral character—that is, agent-evaluations—fell out favor almost completely by the middle decades of the twentieth century in ethics.

This trend flourished in the first half of the twentieth century in the work of philosophers such as G. E. Moore, W. D. Ross, and H. A. Prichard. In the opening of his 1903 *Principia Ethica*, for example, Moore asserted pointedly that "conduct is undoubtedly by far the commonest and most generally interesting object of ethical judgments."[4] The evaluation of actions and their consequences along with principles governing proper conduct had become the fundamental work of philosophical ethics, while the evaluation of agents (people), their motives, and their character receded almost entirely. Conduct, not character, mattered most.

Things began to change in Anglo-American philosophy, however, around the middle of the twentieth century with the publication of Elizabeth Anscombe's landmark article, "Modern Moral Philosophy":

> The concept of obligation, and duty – *moral* obligation and *moral* duty, that is to say – and what is *morally* right and wrong, and of the *moral* sense of "ought," ought to be jettisoned...It would be a great improvement if, instead of "morally wrong," one always named a genus such as "untruthful," "unchaste," "unjust".[5] (Anscombe 1958).

"Untruthful," "unchaste" and "unjust" name traditional vices. Thus Anscombe argues that contemporary philosophical ethics ought to cease describing conduct as morally right and wrong and instead reclaim the vocabulary of vice and virtue.

Anscombe argues that, contrary to the idea that philosophical ethics divorced from God and religion can focus on analysis of observable acts as being morally right or wrong, ethics without God loses all tenable connections to the very concepts of right and wrong in terms of moral duty and obligation. This is so because the concepts of moral obligation, duty, and right conduct are inextricably tied to the concept of *law*, which itself is conceptually bound to the notion of a *lawgiver*. In the absence of a moral lawgiver, in the absence

---

[4] Cambridge University Press, 2.
[5] *Philosophy* 33, No. 124 (January 1958), 1.

of God, the central concepts of modern moral philosophy—concepts of duty, obligation, and right conduct—lose hold. By contrast, concepts of vice and virtue are independent of the concept of moral law. Virtuous character was the concern of Plato and Aristotle, quite independently of God, religion or moral law. That it was also the concern of Aquinas and other Christian thinkers shows that, while concepts of vice and virtue are independent of a theological framework for ethics, they are also quite compatible with one.

In order to understand Anscombe's argument, it is useful to distinguish two different kinds of law. Compare civil law, on the one hand, with the laws of science and logic and the other. The latter are descriptive. They explain how phenomena behave and describe what follows as a logical consequence. Civil law, by contrast, does not describe how citizens do in fact behave. Instead, it prescribes how they should behave. Prescriptive civil law requires a motivational component to ensure as far as possible that people do behave as they should. In civil society, the motivational component is secured by institutions and agents who give and enforce the laws.

When moral philosophy was located squarely within a theological context, the notion of prescriptive moral law made sense. The idea was that, however much philosophy could analyze moral concepts showing them to be intelligible and in accord with reason, moral precepts were in accord with the will of a divine lawgiver and enforcer. As such, the motivational quality of moral injunctions was quite intact, theoretically. Human agents are motivated to act in accord with moral law because it is authorized and ultimately enforced by God. Modern moral philosophy, however, having separated philosophical ethics from notions of divine laws and a divine lawgiver, lost hold of any plausible theoretical ground for the concept of moral law, and concomitant grounds for moral motivation.

Modern moral philosophy seems to have inherited concepts of moral obligation, moral duty, and actions being morally right and wrong from medieval philosophy and theology. Moreover, the notion of a moral law, which the above concepts presuppose, is commensurate with modern scientific modes of intelligibility—in particular the discovery of laws of science. But whatever the historical and intellectual-cultural explanations, Anscombe shows the unintelligibility of modern moral philosophy's treatment of moral motivation within its framework of moral law absent a moral lawgiver. The two most important modern moral theories, the deontology of Kant and the utilitarianism of Bentham, and Mill, each tried to give an adequate account. Each fails, however, according to Anscombe.

Risking oversimplification, it seems fair to say that Kant works out an account of moral law at the expense of a tenable account of moral motivation, while utilitarians work out an account of motivation at the expense of any adequate account of moral law (universality).

Kant (18th century) develops a system of moral imperatives which sought to ground a concept of moral law in reason itself. Much as the laws of logic oblige valid inference, the moral law, according to Kant, obliges correct moral thought and action. As the consequent of a conditional follows logically from the affirmation of its antecedent irrespective of the motivational set of the individual reasoner, so, according to Kant, the moral law compels right conduct irrespective of the motives and desires of individual agents.

Bentham and Mill's (19th century) utilitarianism sought to ground the motivational quality of moral reasoning, as they understood it, in the desires to seek pleasures and avoid pains. On this account the aim of morality is to bring about as much happiness (pleasure) for the greatest number possible. This goal however requires robust egalitarianism, the idea that nobody else's interests count any less than one's own. Thus an action that would make the greatest number of people happy while making oneself miserable is morally obligatory, according to utilitarians. What concept of moral law absent a lawgiver could possibly ground such a universal obligation? Utilitarians seem to try to ground the obligation in naïve optimism in Enlightenment reasonableness: egalitarianism is simply fair, impartial, and non-arbitrary.

For these reasons, then, Anscombe argues that modern moral theories are fundamentally flawed. They base their concepts upon an incoherent notion of a moral "law" without a lawgiver. This leaves us two options: either reconnect morality, conceptually and otherwise, to God and the notion of divine moral commands, or else stop conceiving of ethics fundamentally in terms of moral obligation, moral duty, and morally right and wrong conduct. Because Anscombe believes that the former is not a live option for many philosophers today, she concludes that we would do well to return to Aristotle's approach to ethics wherein the concepts of virtue and character are central. (As noted above, virtue ethics is compatible with God and religion, as it was for Aquinas, though it is also quite independent of them, as it was for Plato and Aristotle.)

There is a second important upshot of Anscombe's article that has implications for the revival of virtue ethics, namely, doubt about the viability of moral theory as such. This theme is picked up in Philippa Foote's "Moral Arguments" (1958; 1978) and "Moral Beliefs" (1959; 1978). By the nineteen-seventies and eighties, a number of articles and books continued the move towards what became known as anti-theory in ethics—the idea that developing a theoretical account of general moral principles and standards for evaluating conduct is not the proper subject matter of philosophical ethics at all. Instead, anti-theorists emphasize the importance of identifying and sorting out the complexity of moral motives, character, and emotions. Philosophical interest in these dimensions of ethical life rather than ethical theory is advanced most notably by Bernard Williams in his critique of utilitarianism (1973), along with his "Morality and Emotions" (1973), "Persons, Character and Morality" (1981), "Moral Luck" (1981), and "Utilitarianism and Self-Indulgence" (1981), and in Michael Stocker's "The Schizophrenia of Modern Ethical Theories" (1976). Williams and Stocker continued their projects in *Ethics and the Limits of Philosophy* (1985) and *Plural and Conflicting Values* (1990), respectively. Also, Alasdair MacIntyre's widely read *After Virtue* (1983) developed many of the same themes from less strictly philosophical and more broadly cultural and historical perspectives.

(A brief caveat is in order here. 'Virtue ethics' may be distinguished from 'virtue theory'. A theory of virtue aims at giving an account of what virtue (or a virtue) is, which traits of character qualify as virtues and what it is about such traits that qualifies them so, along with an account of why these qualities are good for people and whether or not they are the same for all people (Rachels 2003). In the contemporary literature, 'virtue theory' is generally reserved for an account of virtue *within* a moral theory, such as Kant's *Doctrine of Virtue* (Hooker 2000) or consequentialist virtue theories (Driver 2001).)

Moral theory, as it developed in modern moral philosophy and continues today, generally comprises three stages of inquiry. The first and most concrete stage is concerned with particular moral judgments, or the evaluation of specific acts. Here we might seek to determine, for example, whether it is unethical to withdraw medically assisted nutrition and hydration from people diagnosed as being in persistent vegetative states. The second stage of inquiry seeks to identify general moral rules or principles for evaluating the entire class of morally relevant actions. Utilitarianism, for example, formulates and seeks to defend the principle that everyone is morally obligated to act in such ways as will achieve the greatest good for the greatest number. The third stage prescribes the general principle or the characteristic that, according to the theory, any action must possess in order to be morally good, right, permissible, or obligatory. So, following utilitarianism as a theory of morality we arrive for example at the conclusion that it is not unethical to withdraw medically assisted nutrition and hydration from patients if doing so promotes the greatest good for the greatest number.[6]

Virtue ethics, on the other hand, takes a more pluralistic and piecemeal approach. While the evaluation of certain acts or kinds of acts are not irrelevant, such as Aristotle's analysis of the act of throwing precious cargo overboard in bad weather at sea, virtue ethics is also and more primarily concerned with the morally relevant emotions, desires, values, perceptions, attitudes, and choices that go together with and help constitute such actions and their evaluation. Unlike modern moral theory, virtue ethics does not aim for a single moral principle to cover all acts. Instead, it aims for reflective and incisive accounts of the broad range of human activity that falls under the category of ethical life. It aims for this in an effort to advance our understanding of what it takes to live well—and, more importantly, to actually live well. For as Aristotle notes, in ethics we are investigating not in order to understand what virtue is, but in order to become good, since otherwise there would be no benefit from it.

The move away from moral theory and towards the ethics of everyday life—including motives, emotions, character, and relationships—also gained momentum from developments in feminism and feminist philosophy. In 1982, developmental psychologist Carol Gilligan attacked the Kantian-inspired psycho-educational theory of moral development and education advanced by Lawrence Kohlberg, showing that characteristically feminine ways of thinking about ethics in terms of caring relationships had been systematically depreciated or devalued, not only in modern moral philosophy, but in moral psychology as well (Gilligan 1982). In 1992, Alison Jaggar's "Feminist Ethics" faulted traditional Western ethics for failing women in several ways. One of the ways traditional Western ethics fails women, according to Jaggar, is by favoring culturally masculine ways of moral reasoning that emphasize rules, universality, and impartiality over culturally feminine ways of moral reasoning that emphasize relationships, particularity, and partiality. Such culturally masculine ways of moral reasoning are endemic to modern moral theory, while virtue ethics emphasizes particularity and pays attention to ethical problems that arise in private life and personal relationships.

In the past twenty years or so, virtue ethics has burgeoned in Anglo-American analytic philosophy to the point where it now constitutes a third major mainstream approach to normative ethics, the other two being

---

[6] For an extended analysis of the three levels of moral theory see C. E. Harris, *Applying Moral Theories* (Belmont, California: Wadsworth Group, 2002), Ch. 1.

deontology and consequentialism. While the latter are model moral theories in the tradition of modern philosophy, virtue ethics remains effectively non-theoretical or even anti-theoretical in its approach. Of course, there is a sense in which philosophers who make contributions to virtue ethics are theorizing; they bring systematic reflective thinking to bear on the range of human life and activity that fall under the concept of ethics. What they do not attempt, however, is a comprehensive systematic account of all the phenomena falling under the concept. In this too contemporary virtue ethics follows Aristotle, who explains that it is important, and a sign of maturity, not to demand too much precision from ethics, in which what we are after is not theoretical understanding, but an illumination of "things that are so for the most part" (1.III. 1094b13-1095a15).[7]

The revival of virtue ethics can be described as a restoration of interest in a number of topics that once figured prominently in the history of philosophy. These include not only the virtues themselves along with motives and character, but also such topics as friendship, moral education, family life, moral wisdom, and a thick concept of human happiness—as distinguished from, say, the much thinner classical utilitarian concept of happiness as a sort of enjoyment. Moreover, although contemporary virtue ethics is not all "neo-Aristotelian" (Slote 2001), almost any version still has roots in ancient Greek philosophy insofar as it employs the central concepts of *aretē* (meaning virtue or excellence), *phronesis* (correct judgment), and *eudaimonia* (happiness or human flourishing) (Hursthouse 2003).

---

[7] I will usually give Aristotle references in the text as just done. Unless otherwise noted, for *Nicomachean Ethics* I use the translation by David Ross (New York: Oxford University Press, 1992). When I use translations by Joe Sachs or Martin Ostwald, I indicate the translator in a footnote.

Chapter 2

VIRTUE ETHICS

The previous chapter presents reasons for the recent revival of virtue ethics in Anglo-American philosophy. Here a more thoroughgoing account of the nature of virtue ethics is provided.

Arguably the best way to get a handle on virtue ethics is to revisit Aristotle's philosophy. It is beneficial to go back to Aristotle when giving an account of virtue, in particular, since his work on the subject has not been surpassed. In order to appreciate Aristotle on virtue and ethics, it is useful to contrast his views with some of those of modern moral philosophy.

What is ethics? Naturally, many people today would likely answer this question in ways that align with the views of modern moral philosophy. *Ethics is a matter of determining what is right and wrong. Ethics is concerned with making the right moral decisions. Ethics is a study of good and bad conduct.* From this perspective, ethics is concerned primarily with the evaluation of acts and kinds of action. Euthanasia, capital punishment, torture, and genetic testing are just a small sampling of classes of action with which ethics, or at least *morality* is thought to be concerned. Indeed, this view of ethics is now so well-established that it might be a surprise to learn that for some twenty-two centuries, up until the 18th, things were very different. For most of the history of philosophy in the West much of the greatest philosophical thinking about ethics had almost nothing to do with determining which acts and kinds of actions are morally right and wrong. Instead, the fundamental concepts of ethics were virtue, character, excellence, and human flourishing.

Utilitarianism is one prominent modern moral theory. It focuses on moral evaluation of actions vis-à-vis their consequences. It does not concern itself primarily with the moral evaluation of people, their intentions, or their character. The attention to actions and their consequences is meant to model the modern scientific method requiring empirical evidence. Actions and consequences can be observed. Intentions, character and happiness cannot. This gives rise to the idea that it is never appropriate to judge intentions, only actions.

Utilitarianism was originally developed by Jeremy Bentham (1748-1832) and John Stuart Mill (1806-1873). Bentham and Mill were among the most forceful advocates of personal liberty, economic freedom, and the separation of church and state. Their work is important to social and political philosophy, as well as ethics. Utilitarianism sets out the Principle of Utility which holds that actions are morally right insofar as they tend to promote happiness, and wrong insofar as they tend to promote unhappiness. Happiness and unhappiness are defined in the most general and inclusive terms as pleasure and pain respectively. Thus utilitarianism conceives of morality not as a matter of human character and virtue, nor as a matter of divine sanction or religious obligation. Instead, utilitarianism conceives of morality as a matter of utility. Its purpose is its usefulness in promoting human welfare, particularly pleasure and the absence of pain. In contrast to medieval moral theo-philosophy, with its emphasis on divine prohibition and punishment, utilitarianism's claim about the purpose of morality was truly revolutionary. It was indeed a revolution in morality to accompany the cotemporaneous revolutions occurring in government and science.

The second major modern moral theory was developed by Immanuel Kant (1724-1804). In stark contrast to utilitarianism, Kant argues that morality is a system of categorical imperatives commanding acts that are intrinsically good irrespective of the consequences of performing them. For Kant, living morally is primarily a matter of living rationally—not a matter of seeking the greatest pleasure. On Kant's view, we have absolute moral obligations that we are duty-bound to meet. For this reason, Kant's ethical theory is described as deontological—"*deon*" being Greek for "obligation" and "duty."

Categorical imperatives command obligatory behavior as objectively necessary apart from their relation to some further end, such as the amount of happiness or unhappiness they might bring about. The best known formulation of Kant's Categorical Imperative of Morality—the moral principle embedded in Kant's ethical theory—is, *Act only according to that maxim whereby you can at the same time will that it should become a universal law.*

Kant's moral theory is extraordinarily intricate and dense. It is developed not so much for the purpose of deciding which acts are right or wrong as for establishing rational grounds for moral judgments. Our purpose here however is not a careful explication of Kant's theory. Instead we are concerned with how Kant's theory is construed for purposes of applying abstract moral principles to particular acts and kinds of actions. That is, as part of the modern moral project of applying reason to the evaluation of actions.

When attempting to determine whether some action or kind of action is morally right or wrong, Kant's theory requires that we determine whether it is rationally possible to will that the action in question should become a universal law—a rule that all people follow. If not, the act cannot be justified either rationally or morally. A simple but effective example is the act of *cutting to the front of a line*. It is not rationally possible to will that such an act should become a universal law, a rule that everybody follow. For, the very concept of a line entails an ordered sequence, and the practice of line-forming precludes everybody being first at the same time. Not cutting to the front of lines, then, is both rationally and morally obligatory.

We might see utilitarianism as an expression and codification of the new freedoms that came out of the Enlightenment. Kant's moral theory, then, may be viewed as an expression and codification of the responsibilities of the newly emerging civil society. With the rise of the nation state and the merchant class, impersonal transactions and voluntary exchange demanded new rules to govern them. Kant's moral theory generates absolute injunctions against cheating, lying, and stealing—and the new temptations toward such behavior made possible by political, social, and economic development. Of course such actions would be proscribed by law. But Kant's moral theory attempts to show that they are immoral because they are irrational. For civil society to function effectively on a large scale, punishment under the law is insufficient. People must internalize moral obligations and duties as principles of rationality itself.

Utilitarianism and Kantian moral theory have had many forceful critics as well as advocates over the past two hundred years. Certainly disputes over these theories remain lively in contemporary philosophical ethics. Recall however Anscombe's trenchant objection to both of them, outlined in Chapter One: both depend upon a concept of moral law divorced from any plausible concept of a moral lawgiver. It was in the light of this objection—coupled with other philosophers' dissatisfaction with both theories' inability to account for motives—that the recent revival of virtue ethics emerged. It is in view of these developments, then, that we return to Aristotle.

This is not the place for a full consideration of Aristotle's ethics. But an account of his notion of character virtues and their place in moral life is important for understanding the contemporary restoration of virtue ethics. It will help us understand both virtue ethics, and the recent development of virtue epistemology.

Aristotle (384-322 BC) was a student of Plato (428-348 BC) until the latter's death. Plato does not compose a work devoted exclusively to ethics, as Aristotle does. Indeed, Aristotle produced at least two works on ethics: *Nicomachean Ethics* and *Eudemian Ethics*. Plato contends that a study of the sciences, mathematics, and metaphysics are necessary prerequisites for understanding The Good. Science, he thought, is preparatory for ethics.

In his *Republic*, Plato lays out the conditions for a utopian government. He argues that we cannot judge the successes and deficiencies of actual governments if we do not have a clear vision of what the ideal would be. In the context of this discussion, Plato contends that The Good is the cause of all knowledge and truth, and is itself something beyond truth and knowledge. The Good is that from which the objects of knowledge derive not only their knowability, "but their very being and reality; and Goodness is not the same thing as being, but even beyond being, surpassing it in dignity and power" (509b 5-8).[1] Thus The Good for Plato is transcendental, and reflection on the nature of the Good is highly abstract and poetical.

Aristotle departs from Plato. He produces works on physics, zoology, biology, logic, and much else, all quite independently of ethics. For Aristotle ethical inquiry, "does not aim at theoretical knowledge... for we are inquiring not in order to know what virtue is, but in order to become good" (II.2.1103b27-29). That is to say, we pursue philosophical reflection on what is good for human beings not because we want a theory of the nature of The Good, but because we want to live well—because we want to be good at living life. This conception of ethics is far from modern moral notions of promoting the greatest happiness for the greatest number (utilitarianism), or meeting one's absolute moral obligations (Kant).

To understand what it takes to live well, Aristotle begins with what is commonly thought and said about human goods by people who have experience with life and who have been well brought-up. That is, he starts with the conventional views of his reasonable and respectable contemporaries. From there he works philosophically toward a deeper and more refined understanding of what human flourishing requires. It is easy enough to identify a plurality of conventional goods such as friendship, health, pleasure, and

---

[1] I will usually give Plato references in the text as just done. For the *Republic*, I use the translation by Paul Shorey, in Edith Hamilton and Huntington Cairns, eds., *The Collected Dialogues of Plato Including the Letters*, Bolligen Series LXXI (Princeton: Princeton University Press, 1989).

wealth. The more difficult and properly philosophical task, however, is to determine whether some of these goods are more desirable than others, and whether there is a highest good—that is, a good which is desirable for its own sake and not for the sake of some other good, and such that all other goods are desirable for its sake.

Aristotle argues that there is a highest good for human beings. *Eudaimonia* is desirable in itself, and all other goods are desirable for the sake of it. The Greek word "eudaimonia" is often translated into English as happiness. So, we all desire happiness for its own sake. Other goods, such a friends, health, and money are desirable for the sake of happiness. Unfortunately, however, contemporary use of the English word "happiness" is rather banal. It does not adequately convey what Aristotle means by *eudaimonia*. For this reason it is useful to try and think in terms of the Greek. "Eudaimonia" is composed of the Greek *eu* (meaning "well") and *daimon* (meaning "spirit"). Thus, *eudaimonia* means being well in spirit, or well-spirited—being fully alive living well. Some commentators translate *eudaimonia* as flourishing or well-being instead of happiness. Good use can be made of all of these translations.

Aristotle thinks it is obvious that no one tries to live well for the sake of some further goal. Instead, we all desire happiness. All subordinate aims such as health and wealth are sought because we consider them to be conducive to our well-being, not because their achievement or possession constitutes well-being. It is, however, common to mistake pleasure or wealth or something else for the highest good. At the same time, simply naming the highest good and acknowledging that it is happiness is of little value. What is needed philosophically is an account of what happiness consists of. Is it simply the possession of all or some of the various human goods like health, wealth, pleasure, and friends? Aristotle argues that it is not. There is something more to happiness. This "something more" is virtue.

Before turning to what makes *eudaimonia* more than the sum total of subordinate goods, it is worth noting that whereas Aristotle takes it to be obvious that no one tries to live well for the sake of some further goal, many proponents of Judeo-Christian and other religious systems of ethics would reject this view. The addition of divine sanction on human morality, something alien to Aristotle's conception of ethics, sees the promise of the Kingdom of God as the ultimate end of virtuous living. Aristotle's conception of ethics, like politics, however, is concerned entirely with what constitutes flourishing in human society.

What more is there to *eudaimonia*—to flourishing, to living excellently—than the possession of desirable goods? Aristotle's answer to this question brings us in contact with the origin of virtue ethics. He holds that happiness consists of goods which the well-spirited person achieves and bears with *ēthikē aretē* —"virtuous character." If a person possesses desirable human goods but lacks virtuous character, that person is neither living excellently nor enjoying an excellently lived life. A philosophical study of ethics, then, for Aristotle, is concerned with understanding—and, so far as possible, achieving—what makes virtuous character possible, so as to make understanding and achieving human happiness possible.

ĒTHIKE ARETE

"Virtuous character" is the common English translation of *ēthikē aretē*. In translation the order of words is reversed. The Greek *ēthikē* is rendered into English as "character" and *aretē* as "virtue". What's more, the conventional translation reverses the roles of noun and adjective in the original Greek where *aretē* is the noun. Perhaps "character excellence" would be a more perspicacious translation of *ēthikē aretē*. Either way, today virtue ethics is described as character-based ethics and distinguished from the rule-based (deontological) and act-based (utilitarian) ethics of modern moral philosophy. The difference is that the character of people is the primary locus of evaluation for virtue ethics, whereas for modern moral philosophy the primary locus of evaluation is not the person but the act itself—what are its consequences, does it conform to universal laws, etc.

Quite a bit can be lost in translation from *ēthikē aretē* to "virtuous character." The English word "virtue" is derived from the Latin *virtus* which is a rendering of the Greek *aretē*. For one, the word "virtue" is not often used in contemporary colloquial English. When it is used it may seem quaint. Or it may elicit puritanical connotations. Indeed, Victorians used "virtue" as a synonym for sexual virginity. Thus it would be highly unusual for contemporary English speakers to ask whether a certain mechanic or physician deserves our trust, our respect and our business *because of his virtue*. Yet such a question would seem perfectly natural to Plato and Aristotle. Indeed something is lost in language, culture and time when we move from the ancient Greek *aretē* through Latin to the current English word "virtue."

The standard lexicon of ancient Greek derives *aretē* from the name Ares, the god of war. It appears that the word originally denoted *the excellence of a brave and noble warrior.* (We see already how far the Greek concept is from Victorian "virtue.") Recently, however, Joe Sachs has contested the connection to Ares. Sachs contends that *aretē* more likely derives from the verb *arariskein*, which means *to fit* or *to be fitting*.[2] Even so, in the prephilosophical works of Homer *aretē is* used to refer to what is fitting for an aristocrat precisely with regard to militaristic courage. (Indeed, the word *arariskein* may itself derive from *Ares*, since "fitting" here refers to what is fitting for an aristocrat, and *aristos* (best) also derives from *Ares*.) Subsequently, within the structure of the emerging meritocratic *polis*, the term came to signify civic virtue and those qualities that distinguish outstanding citizens, which includes qualities in addition to courage. Eventually, the concept came to refer to an even more generalized quality of *excellence*. In this sense, Plato and Aristotle sought to understand the *aretē* (excellence) of each thing and kind of thing according to its nature. Thus, they could ask what constitutes the excellence of a rose, or a horse, or a man. Regarding the latter, they could ask what constitutes the excellence of a man in his capacity as a mechanic, or in his capacity as a man. (For good reason, then, some commentators prefer "excellence" to "virtue" as a translation of *aretē*.)

This general sense of excellence is the meaning of the term *aretē* employed by Aristotle. The *aretē* of a house builder, for example, is that quality by which he produces good houses. In a bloodhound *aretē* is the quality by virtue of which the animal follows a scent over great distances. A hound that follows a scent tenaciously is *more excellent* vis-à-vis the virtue of a hound than one that quits early, or one that is easily distracted. Further, the *aretē* of a hammer is that which makes it fit to the task of driving nails.[3] A poor hammer, then, lacks *aretē*. It lacks the excellence proper to a hammer: excellent balance, weight, handles' length, tensile strength, and grip. Thus we see that though it would seem odd to complain in current English usage that a poor hammer lacks *virtue*, or to commend a mechanic who is adept at fixing engines as a *virtuous* mechanic, in the sense in which the Greek philosophers use the term, ultimately translated through Latin into English as "virtue," it makes sense entirely.

The *philosophical* sense of *aretē* employed by Plato and Aristotle, then, denotes "the excellence which makes anything an outstanding specimen of its

---

[2] Aristotle, *Nicomachean Ethics*. Translated by Joe Sachs. (Newburyport, MA: Focus Publishing, R. Pullins Co., 2002), 212.

[3] Here I am indebted to Martin Ostwald's translation with introduction and notes of Aristotle's *Nicomachean Ethics* (New York: Bobbs-Merrill Co., 1962), 303.

kind, especially well fitted to its ends."[4] Thus *character* virtue—*ēthikē aretē* —means excellence of character and refers to that quality whereby a human being is especially well fit for human life—for *eudaimonia*, for being well in spirit, for being fully alive living excellently, for happiness.

VIRTUS

Roman and later medieval European translations rendered *aretē* into Latin as *virtus*, derived from the root *vir*, which is the root of the English word "virility." In Latin *vir* means man, manly or soldier. While some five-hundred years passed between Homer and Aristotle, time in which the meaning of the concept *aretē* shifted with developments in Greek culture as noted above, Roman interpretation and Latin translations of the poet and the philosopher were contemporaneous. That is, the Romans interpreted the meanings of *aretē* employed by Homer and Aristotle concurrently. Likewise, later Latin translations simultaneously rendered the earlier Greek concept that denoted military courage and the later Greek concept that denoted the excellence which makes anything an outstanding specimen of its kind as *virtus*—one Roman concept and one Latin term for a putatively unified concept, without regard for the Greek cultural and intellectual developments that shifted the meaning of *aretē* over time.

A hypothetical analogy might help bring out the significance of this. Imagine that modern civilization were set back for the next millennium until a new age of enlightenment rediscovered the great books. Among the collection would be works of Kepler, Newton and Einstein. Now imagine our far in the future cousins translating 'gravitation' in a world in which the significance of the conceptual developments of 'gravitation' between the seventeenth and the twentieth century had been lost. Imagine them attempting to render the concept in a world in which the meanings of inertia and gravitational mass had disappeared. Naturally they would translate the term in whichever way best fit their purposes and understandings. They might take Einstein to be using 'gravitation' in the same sense in which Kepler uses it, as applicable only to bodies at rest. Or, noting differences, they might judge that, whatever Einstein was going on about, it is Kepler who captures the central meaning of gravitation.

---

[4] Sachs, *NE*, 212.

Virtue Ethics   25

We must wonder, then, to what extent the eventual Latin translations blur the development of the concept from the pre-philosophical *excellence of a brave soldier* to the philosophical *excellences of character of a human being which fit him for happiness*. We must further wonder the extent to which the pre-philosophical meanings fit the Roman understanding of civic virtue and excellent character better than the philosophical concept did. In the light of R an appropriation of Greek culture, the Roman concept *virtus*, a concept inherited and developed by medieval Christianity, may well be significantly different from the Greek *philosophical* concept *aretē*. Such a shift or reversal of meaning, moreover, would most certainly affect—or distort—our contemporary concept of moral virtue, such as it is.

The Roman and medieval Christian notions of virtue and character emphasize strength, power, force, and battle in ways alien to Aristotle's concept of *ēthikē aretē*. This is seen in the Stoic and Christian emphasis on the principal importance of *The Will* in moral life; a concept some distance from Aristotle's notion of human goods being objects of *deliberate choice*. For Stoicism, the dominant philosophy of the Roman Empire, *virtus* is the strength to keep one's will in accord with nature. A vivid picture of Stoic virtue is painted by a passage from the private notebook of the Roman emperor Marcus Aurelius Antoninus (121-180 AD):

> Begin the morning by saying to yourself, I shall meet with the busy-body, the ungrateful, arrogant, deceitful, envious, unsocial. All these things happen to them by reason of their ignorance of what is good and evil. But I who have seen the nature of the good that it is beautiful, and of the bad that it is ugly, and the nature of him who does wrong, that it is akin to me, not only of the same blood or seed, but that it participates in the same intelligence and the same portion of the divinity, I can neither be injured by any of them, for no one can fix on me what is ugly, nor can I be angry with my kinsman, nor hate him. For we are made for co-operation, like feet, like hands, like eyelids, like the rows of the upper and lower teeth. To act against one another then is contrary to nature; and it is acting against one another to be vexed and to turn away.[5]

It is as natural for human beings to cooperate in civic life as it is natural for birds to nest. Yet, uncooperative people are found everywhere. A virtuous Stoic, however, is one who has the strength of will and character not be vexed

---

[5] Quoted in Wallace Matson, *A New History of Philosophy: Volume One: From Thales to Ockham* (Orlando, FL: Harcourt, Inc., 2000), 189.

by the uncooperative behavior of people who are ignorant of what is natural and good. Instead, a virtuous citizen, much like a good soldier, perseveres with equanimity.

Further, in the milieu of early Christian society the Hebrew notion of divine command over human morality fused with the Greek notion of virtuous character. Thus Augustine (354-430 AD) adds to ethics the concept of a personal God, free-will, and sin. The result is a conception of moral virtue as *strength of will aided by the grace of God*. Today our ordinary understanding of moral virtue, such as it is, remains shaped by the Latinized and Christianized conception of moral virtue. It is, however, a conception of virtue far removed from Aristotle's notion of *ēthikē aretē*—that excellence of character whereby a human being is well fit for happiness. Yet it is to Aristotle's notion that contemporary philosophy, and virtue ethics and virtue epistemology in particular, returns.[6]

PSYCHE

Characterological virtue is a stable condition. It is a posture, a matter of how one comports oneself in the world. It is not an action, nor a way of acting. It is a way of being. While it is true that people who possess virtuous character behave and act in characteristically virtuous ways, non-virtuous people may act virtuously without being virtuous. Performing actions that a virtuous person would perform does not make one virtuous.

Aristotle defines excellences of character— *ēthikē aretē* —as *hexeis* of the rational soul by which one consistently chooses the mean in matters of feeling and action, knowingly and for its own sake (1105a30-33, 1106b36-1107a2). Before we unpack this crucial definition and the meaning of the term *hexis*, it will be useful to consider first what Aristotle means by the soul. For character virtue and happiness are, according to Aristotle, conditions of the soul. It is for this reason that we say that a person may perform acts that a virtuous person would perform without being virtuous, insofar as he lacks a virtuous soul.

Aristotle's notion of the soul develops out of his inquiries into nature in general and its principles (metaphysics), and into the physical universe and its structure (physics). His conception of the soul is also shaped by his

---

[6] I thank William V. Rowe for helpful discussion here. Rowe points to Nietzsche's *Prefaces of Unwritten Works* and Heidegger's *The Fundamental Concepts of Metaphysics: World, Finitude, Solitude* for corroboration that Roman interpretations and later medieval Christian translations distort Greek philosophy significantly

investigations in botany and zoology. Thus, Aristotle's account of the soul is an upshot of his work in the sciences, not theology, about which Aristotle says comparatively little. Aristotle's physical and metaphysical inquiries are primarily concerned with the beings that are in the universe. In his investigations into the nature of beings, of what it is to be, Aristotle distinguishes the being of animate and inanimate things.

Aristotle analyzes each thing into a union (*synolon*) of material and form. The form is the source which makes something the kind of thing it is. Thus the definitions of genera are definitions of the common form of the species that fall under each genus. The material of each thing is the source by virtue of which, in receiving the form, a thing is *an individual*, or some *this*. Thus Iceland-moss and mountain moonwort, for example, may be comprised of basically the same material (cellulose, carbon, hydrogen, nitrogen, etc.), but they belong to different genera—moss and fern, respectively—by virtue of their different forms. By 'form' Aristotle does not mean merely the gross shape of a thing, but, for living things, the structural organization of material directing development in such a way as to make a thing the kind of thing it is. (Today, regarding animate objects, we might liken Aristotle's conception of form to our understanding of the dynamism of genetic code or information.) The form and material of beings in the universe are never separate, but unified and inseparable in each thing. That is to say, each thing is precisely a composite of form and material. We distinguish the two only conceptually.

Living things, then, are composed of the two principles form and matter. The forms of living things possess the special characteristics by which they are living (or *animate*), as opposed to inanimate. This particular kind of form Aristotle designates as the animate thing's *psychē,* or soul. This noun, which is derived from the verb *psychō* (to breathe) has as its original meaning breath. Other meanings of *psychē* include life, spirit, and mind. Aristotle uses *psychē* in a technical sense to refer specifically to the form of a living body.

The souls of all animate beings must at least have a vegetative character. (The term "vegetative" is derived from the Latin *vegetus*, which means "with life.") The vegetative or nutritive soul refers to that by which living bodies assimilate nutrients from the environment, grow, and reproduce. This nutritive power exhausts the soul of plants. To contemporary readers a passing reference to "the souls of plants" may seem far-fetched. Recall, though, for Aristotle *psychē* refers to the principle of animation of living bodies. It does not refer in the first instance to anything we might call spiritual. Indeed, it would be absurd to suggest that today we have a firm grasp of the meaning of the term 'soul', and that it certainly excludes the principle of life at work in plants. On the contrary, Aristotle's analysis of the concept 'soul' seems much clearer and more precise than contemporary uses of the term which seem to derive from a conceptual muddle of ambiguity, vagueness, and inconsistency.

Unlike plants, other animate beings exhibit powers of sensation and locomotion. Aristotle attributes to such animals the powers of a sentient soul. (The term "sentient" derives from the Latin *sentire,* which means "to feel.") Human animals exhibit powers of abstract thinking. Aristotle attributes to us the powers of an intellectual or rational soul, including the power of conceptual reasoning. Hence the nutritive soul (its powers, properties, functions) names the form of plants; the nutritive + sensitive soul names the form of non-human animals; and the nutritive + sensitive + rational soul names the form of human beings. A human being is a more complex soul than a plant, but the powers of the human soul include both sentient and vegetative functions, the latter in common with plants.

The Latin translation of *psychē* is *anima,* which has the same range of meanings. In the Latin vocabulary, then, we find the word *animal* which means "a living thing." Latin is the source of the English terms "animate" and "inanimate"—describing things which have or do not have *anima,* a living form.

The term *psychē is* the source of the English noun "psychology," meaning the study of the mind. When Aristotle investigates the nature of soul in "On the *Psychē,*" however, he is not concerned with psychology in the modern academic or clinical sense. He is investigating epistemology—and in particular, how human beings acquire knowledge. For Aristotle, knowledge is a condition of the soul (which is to say, of the person), not a mental state (which is to say, a condition of the mind.) Following the mind/body dualism of Descartes, many modern philosophers conceive of knowledge as a relation between ideas in the mind and objects in the world. On this view, knowledge is (wrongly) pictured as a mental state—the state of having or holding certain ideas in the mind.

American philosopher Charles Sanders Peirce (1839-1914) offers a thoroughgoing repudiation of the modern philosophical notion of knowledge in terms of ideas in the mind. While an account of Peirce's arguments goes beyond our present purposes, let it suffice to say that his work in semiotics and logic show that the very notion of "ideas in the mind" is misconceived. Knowing, he argues, is a future-directed inferential process involving signs. We can only access our own thoughts indirectly through their external aspects, through that at which our thought-signs point. That is, we can only access our thoughts through their objects. Though philosophy, linguistics, and psychology have moved on from the modern view of thought and knowledge in terms of ideas in the mind, this false picture still colors ordinary speech and folk psychology. We are still inclined to think of ourselves as thinking vis-à-vis "our minds" and their "ideas." As a result, we are in a position to misunderstand Aristotle when he claims that virtue is a stable condition of the *psychē*. We might think he means that virtue is a condition of "the mind" in terms of some misconceived picture of the mind, or that virtue is a condition of "the soul" in terms of some misconceived picture of the soul.

When Aristotle defines *ēthikē aretē* as *hexeis* of the rational soul, he defines virtuous character as a stable condition of the whole person in possession of intelligence. Virtuous character refers to the stable condition of a rational person as the deliberative source of his thoughts, feelings, and actions wherein he chooses the mean knowingly and for its own sake. These choices, acts, feelings and thoughts are not mental activities in the modern sense, but activities of persons. Indeed, achieving and being in such stable active conditions of the soul is, for Aristotle, *being fully alive*.

HEXEIS

Virtues of character are active conditions of a rational soul by which a person consistently chooses the mean, knowingly and for its own sake, in matters of feeling and action (1105a30-33, 1106b36-1107a2). By feelings Aristotle means "desire, anger, fear, confidence, envy, joy, affection, hatred, yearning, jealousy, pity, and generally those things which are accompanied by pleasure or pain" (1105b22-24).[7] Virtues are "the active conditions in accordance with which we bear ourselves well or badly toward the feelings; for example, in relation to being angry, if we are that way violently or slackly, we bear ourselves badly, but if in a measured way, we bear ourselves well, and similarly in relation to other feelings" (1105b26-30).[8]

A virtue is not itself a feeling or an action. It is an active condition of the soul, a *hexis*. A *hexis* is "any way in which one deliberately holds oneself in relation to feelings and desires…, once it becomes a constant part of oneself" (NE 1105b 25-26).[9] *Hexis* is often (mis)translated from Greek through Latin to English as "habit." The English word "habit," however, not only fails to

---

[7] Sachs, *NE*, 27.
[8] Ibid.
[9] Sachs, *NE*, 201.

30   Daniel P. Haggerty

capture the meaning of *hexis;* the mistranslation ultimately leads to confusing
Aristotle's *ēthikē aretē* with "moral virtue."

The word *ēthikē* is derived from the word *ēthos* (with a long e; that is,
with an eta). In ancient Greek, *ēthos* means character. The word *ethos* (with a
short e; that is, with an epsilon), on the other hand, means habit. Aristotle
contends that excellent character comprises *hexeis*. According to recent
commentary by Sachs, the Greek word *hexis* is routinely mistranslated into
English as "habit" as a result of a Latin translation of Aristotle which Aquinas
read and commented upon in the 13th century.[10] In this translation the Latin
word *habitus* (English "habit") is used for the Greek *hexis*. Thus we inherit the
mistaken notion that excellent character is a matter of possessing the right
habits. Further, in Latin habits are *mōrēs*, from which we derive the English
word "moral." Hence the English expression "moral virtue"—which, as noted
above, suggests something like *strength of will produced by good habits and
God's grace*. This concept is *not* what Aristotle means by *ēthikē aretē*.

Conceptual distance and mistranslation result in the misconception that
Aristotle claims that excellence of character consists of good habits. A habit is
something done because it has been done many times before. As Sachs
explains, "The study of ethics (for Aristotle) is about the things that have to do
with character (*ēthos*), not about socially approved habits, or habits of any
kind. Character consists of active conditions, which are not habits, though they
require habits as preconditions" (1179b 23-26).[11] Thus, in order to understand
Aristotle's analysis of virtue we must distinguish active conditions (*hexeis*)
from the habits they require.

Hexeis are active conditions of the soul. They require habits, which is to
say that they are the result of training and conditioning. But whereas mere
habitual behaviors are passive, *hexeis* and behavior that spring from them are
active. A *hexis* is "any condition that a thing has by its own effort of holding
on in a certain way."[12] Some *hexeis* are active conditions of the body, not of
character. Take breathing as an example. We can draw an illuminating analogy
between the *hexis* by which a certain excellence of breathing is achieved and
the *hexeis* by which excellence of character is achieved.

Recall that excellences of character involve thoughts, feelings, and
actions. Like breathing, we all think, feel, and act. We may think, feel, act, and
breathe passively, of necessity. Or we may acquire active conditions towards

---

[10] Sachs, *NE*, xi-xvii.
[11] Sachs, *NE*, 206.
[12] Aristotle's *Metaphysics*. Translated by Joe Sachs. (Santa Fe, NM: Green Lion Press, 2002),
xlix).

Virtue Ethics 31

these activities. A breath-hold underwater diver must train holding breath. He must condition himself. One technique requires holding breath at rest for some time, and then walking as far as possible without breaking the hold. This is an example of acquiring an active condition with respect to breathing, or not breathing. It requires holding on in a certain way, which is markedly different from passive breathing. Excellent breath-hold divers can hold breath and swim more than one-hundred twenty meters without fins.

For excellence in breath-hold diving, training is required and breath-hold habits must be formed. The breath-hold dive, however, is an active condition of the diver, of his thoughts, feelings, and actions, and of his body and breath. The breath hold is not a habit. Training and habit formation are required, but the breath-hold diver while diving is doing more than acting habitually. He is actively holding an ongoing state in a certain way. This is what Aristotle means by *hexis*.

Like an excellent breath-hold, the excellence of character related to anger requires training. It requires habits of thought, feeling and action with respect to anger and occasions for anger. But the virtue of character with respect to anger itself is something more than a habit. It is a condition of a person who, by his own effort, holds on in a certain way with respect to his thoughts, feelings, and actions in conditions that call for anger. He holds on in a certain way—neither losing control nor backing off. As such, the person of virtuous character with respect to anger gets angry "with the people whom one ought to get angry with, on the grounds on which one ought, as one ought" (1126b7-9).

A person might develop good habits (*ethos*) with respect to fear, such as breathing slower and magnifying his sense of competence while minimizing vulnerability and danger. But the character (*ēthos*) virtue (*aretē*) courage is not identical to the set of such habits, however helpful they may be in acquiring and sustaining the virtue. Instead, the excellence or virtue courage is, like all virtues, a *maximum condition* (1106b36-1107a8) in which all the human powers of thought, feeling, and desire are present and working together in harmony (1139a 22-26, b 4-5). Obviously, it is possible to possess the relevant good habits without having achieved the maximum condition as a stable condition of soul. But it is the possession of such maximum conditions that is constitutive of *eudaimonia*—being fully alive living well.[13] (Julia Annas

---

[13] For a phenomenology of how it feels to be excellent, to live well, see Julia Annas, The Structure of Virtue. In *Intellectual Virtue*. edited by DePaul and Zagsebski (Oxford: Oxford University Press, 2003), 15-33.

provides a phenomenology of the unique feel of living excellently; Annas, 2008.)

Virtues of character are not just any kind of active condition. As we have seen, breath-holding is an active condition of the body, but not a character virtue. Moreover, it is possible that non-human animals, such as well-trained well-bred dogs, may possess and exercise certain excellences. But these are not excellences of character. Virtues of character require deliberative choice, a rational power. Such virtues are active conditions of the soul by which a person discerns and chooses the mean in feeling and action for its own sake. To choose the mean is to deliberate and decide in such a way as to be or to remain self-poised. The mean is the balanced choice of feeling and action, chosen knowingly and for its own sake. Something is chosen for its own sake when it is sought as desirable and good in itself, and not as an instrument to some other good. People who are still learning to be virtuous may choose the mean for the sake of honor, or out of shame, or even from ignorance. By contrast, to choose the mean in feeling and action for its own sake is to choose it for the sake of feeling and acting well, or beautifully.

SOME VIRTUES AND VICES OF CHARACTER

Every virtue of character, according to Aristotle, is a reliable capacity to discern and choose the mean—that which is in no way excessive or deficient in relation to the relevant feelings and actions. Temperance, for example, names the virtue by which one discerns and chooses the actions and feelings conducive to and constitutive of bodily pleasures. Discerning and choosing the mean in this context is choosing bodily pleasures in the ways and to the extent that they enhance life. This is another way of saying, bodily pleasures chosen knowingly and for the sake of feeling and acting beautifully. Hence, choosing the mean is not a matter of moderation or self-control, where feelings and desires remain excessive or deficient. Rather, the virtue temperance is marked by harmony of desire and reason in a stable active condition of the soul (1119a 11-20). A temperate person knows how to choose bodily pleasures in ways and to the extent that they enhance life, and desires such pleasures and the feelings and actions that accompany and perfect them.

The temperate person's desire for pleasures is robust without being excessive. The man whose desire for pleasures is excessive but suppressed may refrain from feeling and acting excessively. But such a man is only exercising self-control. Self-control is not a virtue. It is not constitutive of

Virtue Ethics

eudaimonia. Courage and temperance are character virtues. Together they ameliorate the various excesses and deficiencies of feeling, desire and action that are characteristic of childhood (1179b29-1180a1).[14] Adults who lack courage or temperance, then, are, in these ways, childish. By contrast, in Plato's *Symposium* Alcibiades describes Socrates at Potidaea: "When we were cut off from our supplies and forced to go without food, as is common on military campaigns, no one else endured it well. But when there was plenty to eat, he alone was really able to enjoy it" (219e8220a2). Here we have a description of a courageous and temperate man whose desires and pleasures are robust.

Self-control is not a virtue; nor is it a vice. We can fall short of virtuous character without being vicious. A vice is a stable condition of the soul whereby a person chooses extremes of excess or deficiency in feeling and action for their own sake (1105a 30-33, 1107a 2-6, 1152a 4-6).[15] Dissipation, for example, names the vice of excess with regard to pleasures of the body. A vice is not an action but a "formed state of character, deliberately chosen, blamable finally because it prevents all the powers within the human soul from coming into any sort of internal harmony" (1166b11-29).[16] Self-control in the place of temperance, then, is a way of holding on to excessive feeling and desire with respect to bodily pleasures. The self-controlled person does not choose the extreme, but neither does he choose the mean for its own sake. He may choose the mean, or he may choose to abstain, for the sake of shame or honor—for the sake of not acting foolishly, which is not the same as choosing the mean for the sake of feeling and acting beautifully. And while choosing not to act foolishly may keep a man from vice, it is not constitutive of *eudaimonia.*

Not all character virtues concern serious matters, like courage and temperance do. As Aristotle notes in *Nicomachean Ethics* 1127b34-1128a6,

> Since in life there is also relaxation, and in this there is a playful way of passing the time, here too there seems to be a harmonious way of associating with people—sorts of things that one ought to say, and a way of saying them, and likewise a way of taking what is said…. And it is clear that in connection with these things too there is an excess and a deficiency with respect to a mean.[17]

---

[14] Sachs *NE*, 211.
[15] Sachs, *NE*, 212.
[16] Ibid.
[17] Sachs, *NE*, 76f.

34 Daniel P. Haggerty

Pleasures and amusement in conversation and social life are human goods. They are part of living well, part of what makes happy lives good. Names for the relevant virtues involved include "wit" and "charm." Buffoonery, a vice, names the stable condition of the soul by which a person desires amusement in conversation too much, and chooses the excess in feelings and actions with respect to such pleasures. This vice characteristically manifests in antics and coarse jokes, or in other ways of *trying* to be funny. There is also a corresponding vice of deficiency. Boorishness is marked by interpersonal dullness, charmless social ignorance and awkwardness. As Aristotle explains, "the boorish person is useless in this sort of social life, for while contributing nothing he is disdainful toward everything" (1128b2f).[18]

Friendliness is another character virtue. Like wit and charm, it concerns the thoughts, feelings and actions that are constitutive of a good and pleasant social life. Friendly people achieve the mean for its own sake with respect to complying with others in words and deeds (1126b12-1127a13).[19] Obsequiousness names the correlative vice of excess. Obsequious people are slavish, being too compliant with the will or wishes of others. They "compliment everything in order to please, and object to nothing, but believe that they must not be responsible for any pain to those they happen to be around" (1126b13-16).[20] Cantankerousness names the correlative vice of deficiency. Cantankerous people are ill-natured and quarrelsome. They object to everything and do not consider at all the pain they cause. They are unwilling to comply. All four of the vices mentioned here are excesses or deficiencies with respect to social pleasures and the knowledge, feelings and actions that enhance social life and make it good.

Finally, being vicious, being virtuous, and being in between are all ultimately up to us, according to Aristotle. That is not to say that circumstances and other people play no role in the development of our character, for good or ill. They certainly do. For the Greeks, "up to us" would not suggest an entirely individual matter. The idea of go-it-alone boot-strap individualism is a fairly recent conception of responsibility. Still, Aristotle is firm that vice and virtue are matters of deliberation and choice. Bad habits and aiming at the wrong things, such as the expedient rather than the beautiful, are the accretion of so many bad choices over time. Of course, people who have acquired truly bad character may seem to be ignorant and unable to choose the mean in feeling and action. Such a condition, however, is a condition of the

---

[18] Sachs, *NE*, 77.
[19] Sachs, *NE*, 73f.
[20] Sachs, *NE*, 74.

soul that is the outcome of decisions that were originally voluntary. Again, the relevant voluntary decisions are not always made by the person whose character is, or is becoming, malformed. As is the case with children, such decisions may also be the responsibility of other people, especially parents and teachers. So whether we achieve excellence and eudaimonia is ultimately up to us, but not simply up to each person individually.

Aristotle draws an analogy between the development of bad character and bad health. "While no one blames those who are ill-formed by nature, people do censure those who are that way through lack of exercise and neglect" (1114a26-28).[21] Passivity and carelessness result in bad character, as they do bad health. Our potential for character virtue must be exercised and developed with deliberation and care. When we neglect to be deliberative about how we feel, what we desire, and how we act, we form bad habits. The result is a condition of soul short—potentially far short—of happiness. Passivity and bad habits harden. The result is disharmonious, or worse, vicious character—an utter lack of self-poise. With this in mind, Aristotle suggests that a person would have to be unconscious not to realize the consequences of living badly. A person would have to be not conscious of his life and choices.

---

[21] Sachs, *NE*, 46.

Chapter 3

FROM HUME TO QUINE: THE SEPARATION OF ETHICS AND EPISTEMOLOGY AND THE RISE OF ANALYTIC PHILOSOPHY

Chapters one and two explored the revival and the nature of virtue ethics. This chapter explores the separation of ethics and epistemology in modern philosophy—a separation that has lasted some three hundred years. The separation is attributed to the philosophy of David Hume, to the rise of the modern scientific method and the concomitant rejection of teleological explanations of natural phenomena, and to developments in the philosophy of mathematics.

DAVID HUME

Over the course of the Enlightenment philosophical ethics not only became secular, it was also sheared away from epistemology. There are many ways of telling this story, but it is most illuminating to turn to the work of David Hume (1711-1776). In *A Treatise on Human Nature*, Hume argues that there is a deep dichotomy—a logical gap—between theoretical judgments that are expressed in descriptive statements of fact and practical judgments that are expressed in prescriptive statements about what ought to be done. Hume's thesis is referred to as the "is/ought distinction" which implies a "fact/value gap."

One upshot of Hume's analysis is that scientific statements and theories, which contain theoretical judgments and assertions of fact, are logically independent of normative statements and theories about what ought to be, including putative assertions about how human beings ought to behave morally. It is one thing to point out facts about human psychology or the human condition, for example, and quite another to claim that people ought to behave in conformity with those facts. Suppose for example that it is a fact that most people tend to care more about the suffering of other people who look like them. Hume would argue that it does not follow from this fact about human psychology that a group of people who look alike *ought* to be relatively unmoved morally by the suffering of people who do not look like members of the group.

A second consequence of Hume's analysis is that the apprehension of facts about the world supplies absolutely no motivation to act or to refrain from acting one way or another. In other words, facts do not provide us with a reason for acting. Since facts about the world are the purview of scientific inquiry, it follows that scientific knowledge cannot give us reasons for acting. Correlatively, our reasons for acting, including our moral reasons, cannot be based on facts. Instead, Hume argues, human motivation is always based on human desire. Our desires condition our reasons for acting, including moral reasons, and desires are not entailed by facts.

Hume attributes the fact/value dichotomy to a distinction in grammar, a change in syntax. He writes,

> In every system of morality, which I have hitherto met with, I have always remark'd, that the author proceeds for some time in the ordinary way of reasoning, and establishes the being of a God, or makes observations concerning human affairs; when of a sudden I am surpriz'd to find, that instead of the usual copulations of propositions, *is*, and *is not*, I meet with no proposition that is not connected with an *ought*, or an *ought not*. This change is imperceptible; but is, however, of the last consequence.[1]

And then, stunningly:

---

[1] David Hume, *A Treatise of Human Nature* (2nd edition). Text revised and notes by P. H. Nidditch. (Oxford: Oxford University Press, 1992), 468-469.

> I am persuaded, that this small attention wou'd subvert all the vulgar systems of morality, and let us see, that the distinction of vice and virtue is not founded merely on the relations of objects, nor is perceiv'd by reason.[2]

Based on the above noted syntactic distinction, a distinction in the logical structure of language, Hume infers that "ought" statements (the purview of ethics) cannot be derived from "is" statements (empirical descriptions or statements of fact). Hume concludes that reason is only suited for judgments concerning what is and what is not the case (facts). It is not suited for deciding what ought and what ought not to be done.

Hume's argument reinforces a theme that developed in the philosophical tradition in the West, and one that is still with us to some extent today. Namely, that it is possible and illuminating to separate a cognitive side of human life from a non-cognitive, affective side. Reason, explanation, and description are thought to belong to the former, while emotion, desire, and motives are supposed to belong to the latter. Science and knowledge go with reason while ethics, following Hume, goes with sentiment.

In the heady days of early 20th century philosophy when the structure of logic and language was thought to mirror the structure of thought and reality, Hume's syntactical distinction, his "logical gap," was construed as showing that *is statements* are about the world, the facts, the way things are, while *ought statements* are about subjective desires, preferences, and sentiments. The effect of Hume's distinction on analytic philosophers was a dichotomizing of moral language from the empirical and inferential language of the sciences and the world they describe. Though Wittgenstein would later argue that grammatical differences are not based on realities that lie behind them, but that they rather direct and express our interests (a thesis one can imagine Hume relishing), Hume's observations were initially taken—and, perhaps, with a drop of subversive irony, intended by Hume to be taken—as *essential* matters involving the *strongest possible necessity*—the distinction between "is" and "ought" indicating a mutually exclusive disjunction separating ethics from serious epistemology and empirical science.

Hume's arguments and the responses they garnered spring from Enlightenment conceptions of science and the nature of scientific inquiry, including conceptions and presuppositions about the power of science and scientific explanation. They are also set against historical exigencies in the Catholic Church, including the rise of Protestantism and the Counter

---

[2] Hume, *Treatise*, 469-470.

Reformation, as well as the role of religion in political and social life. In this context Hume aims to show that science is, in the strictest possible terms, distinct from morality. Against the dogma of a morally ordered reality discernible by privileged reason and every bit as "factual" and "lawful" as the world that science studies, Hume argues that morality is comprises nothing more than human passion and feelings.

A close reading of Hume, however, shows him to be every bit as derisive about the pretenses of science as he is about the pretensions of moralists. For Hume, passion and subjectivity are not sullied things inferior to the clean, clear work of cognition in science. Rather, human feeling and desire are the wellsprings of human freedom, both individual and political. Instead of being oppressed by the philosopher, the theologian, and the man of science, with their seductive appeals to universal truths, hard facts, and unyielding objectivity, both the individual and society are empowered, liberated, and enriched by human passion. By arguing that there are no moral facts as there are natural facts, Hume does not mean to be dooming ethics. Instead, he means to direct moral and political inquiry away from dogma and toward the creation of a more open, tolerant, liberal democratic society.

Nevertheless, Hume's arguments were hijacked by subsequent thinkers who viewed modern science as *terra firma*—a system of justified true beliefs based upon foundational observation statements inoculated against any threat of skepticism. From *this* perspective, rather than Hume's, since the value and power of science alone are incontrovertible, and ethics is not science, ethics itself is controverted. Not only are all particular ethical judgments arguable, moral considerations themselves are always beside the point from an intellectual, which is to say scientific, point of view.

NATURAL LAW

Though Hume does not identify the "vulgar systems of morality" that he has in mind when he accuses them of illicitly inferring "ought" (prescriptive) statements from "is" (descriptive) statements, natural law theory is unquestionably a primary target of his criticism. Natural law theory in ethics is committed to epistemological naturalism concerning moral knowledge. This is the view that practical reasoning—which includes ethical reasoning, and is distinguished from theoretical reasoning—employs the usual methods for gaining knowledge of the natural world, such as observation and induction. That is, moral knowledge is acquired in much the same way as empirical knowledge in the natural sciences. This view is contrasted with Hume's position on the one hand, according to which morality is a matter of sentiment, not knowledge, and with Plato's on the other, according to which knowledge of the good requires transcendental intuition.

Natural law theories of ethics have been attributed to Aristotle, the Stoics, Cicero, and Hobbes. But the ethical theory of the 13th century Dominican priest, philosopher and theologian Thomas Aquinas (1225-1274) is the standard of natural law ethics against which Hume is reacting. This is not to say that Hume argues against Aquinas directly, or exclusively. Instead, Hume had in his sights the five hundred year tradition of natural law ethics running from Aquinas through successors, including the early 17th century Jesuit Spanish priest, philosopher and theologian Francisco Saurez.

Aquinas' natural law theory of ethics was absorbed and widely circulated throughout the Catholic Church in Europe over the five centuries from Aquinas to Hume. It was the predominant theory of philosophical and theological ethics of the time. Natural law remains the principal moral theory of the Roman Catholic Church today, albeit with important modifications since the 13th century. At bottom, natural law ethics contends that there are basic goods grounded in and derived from human nature. Actions that promote basic goods are morally right, and actions directly aimed at bringing about the opposite of basic goods are morally wrong. In this way natural law does seem to require what Hume finds impossible; namely, that we derive what ought and ought not to be done from facts about human nature.

(Recall that Elizabeth Anscombe argues that modern moral theories are based on an incoherent notion of moral law absent a moral lawgiver, and that therefore ethics should either return to a theistic worldview or else reorganize around Aristotle's pre-Christian notion of virtue (*aretē*). She considers a philosophical return to theistic ethics unlikely, which is why she recommends revisiting the ancient concepts of vice and virtue instead. Still, some version of Aquinas' natural law theory would seem to be a viable option for philosophers who do not reject out of hand the notion of philosophical ethics in a theistic context.)

For Aquinas, laws of physics, cosmology and the rest of what we call natural science are of a piece with natural moral laws. In the most general sense a law, according to Aquinas, is a rule of action put into place by one who has authority in the community (*ST* IaIIae).[3] On this definition, then, the laws

---

[3] I will usually give references to Aquinas' *Summa Theologica* in the text as just done. I use the English translation by the Fathers of English Dominican Province, in three volumes (New York: Benzinger Bros., 1947).

of science are precisely the rules of inquiry agreed upon by the scientific community. Since, in Aquinas' view God has ultimate authority and care of the universe, "eternal law" refers to the rules of action put into place by God in creation. Eternal law refers to the rational plan by which all of nature is ordered (*ST* IaIIae). So for Aquinas and the medieval Christian worldview, principles of matter and motion, for example, are aspects of the eternal law of God.

Natural law, then, refers to one aspect of divine providence contained and expressed in eternal law. Specifically, natural law is the way in which human beings, equipped with intellect and will, uniquely "participate" in the eternal law (*ST* IaIIae). Human beings can act freely in accordance with principles of reason. By doing so we contribute to and help bring about God's plan. Other creatures are subject to eternal law, but lacking a rational nature and participation in the eternal law, they are causally determined by nature. On this view, both laws of science and laws of morality are expressions of divine providence.

It was precisely this view that was challenged and ultimately overturned by modern science. Even while many of the scientists of the modern era seem to have been theists or deists, they developed a methodology and an outlook that sidelined God as the author of nature. This move was of course essential in at least one important respect. The prior medieval policy of taking theology as Queen of the Sciences meant that scientific findings had to avoid conflict with scripture, doctrine, and dogma. The rise of modern science was made possible in no small part as a result of emancipation from this stultifying mandate.

Eventually scientism—the view that science alone can render truth—in analytic philosophy appropriated epistemology. The theory of knowledge was reduced to theory of scientific knowledge. Indeed, the very idea of non-scientific knowledge, such as moral knowledge, came to be regarded as untenable. If morality is concerned with feeling and desire while science is concerned with facts, epistemology is concerned with science. By the early twentieth century in Anglo-American philosophy, religion is consigned to myth and ethics is demoted to mere passion.

TELEOLOGY

Hume identifies a logical gap between descriptive (scientific) statements and prescriptive (ethical) statements. Early analytic philosophers take this to imply that knowledge is restricted to descriptive statements. It was in this vein that, in the nineteen twenties and early nineteen thirties, logical positivists held that knowledge was restricted to observation statements plus mathematical and logical propositions. The latter were not thought to produce knowledge of the world, but are nevertheless necessary to reduce meaningful theoretical statements to basic observation statements. Thus logical positivism (also known as logical empiricism) restricts knowledge to science and regards ethics, religion, aesthetics, and metaphysics as pseudo-subjects about which we cannot speak meaningfully.

Positivists considered their views to be in line with Hume's. However, Hume himself contends that science does not produce knowledge of the world. Indeed, in the *Treatise of Human Nature* Hume reduces the world, the object of scientific investigation, to a mere complex of sensations. Objective knowledge is nothing more than a wish, according to Hume, in ethics and science. Knowledge is restricted to one's own impressions. The route from Hume's skepticism to scientism, to the reduction of epistemology to knowledge in the sciences, runs through the emergence of the modern view of scientific explanation as entirely mechanistic—and thus non-teleological.

It would be a mistake to think that the debate over teleological and mechanistic explanations of nature is a uniquely modern concern. To the contrary, Aristotle argues against the atomistic materialism of his predecessors. According to Aristotle, adequate explanation and knowledge of nature require both mechanical and teleological principles.

Teleology (from the Greek *telos*, meaning 'an end') is the explanation or interpretation of natural phenomena in the light of the concept of final causes. Final causes are distinguished from efficient causes insofar as the latter are conceived of as *prior* causal conditions and the former as *posterior* causal conditions. Though final causes of natural phenomena are often portrayed as external ends, especially by modern thinkers who reject the notion of final causes, Aristotle's conception of ends includes a concept of organic final cause. On this view biological organization and function are explained in part by the end or complete form of organism toward which the biological activity is directed. Today, though putative explanations of natural phenomena in terms of *external* final causes do seem to be non-scientific, it is not entirely clear that a concept of internal ends is not necessary for adequate explanation of functional biology. Moreover, though arguments for the existence of God based on alleged evidence of design in the cosmos are also non-scientific "explanations" of natural phenomena in terms of external ends, evidence of a cosmos finely tuned for life does seem to constitute grounds for an internal principle or principles of cosmic organization that are teleological in nature.

Ancient atomists Leucippus and Democritus (5th century BC) held a materialist view of nature and a mechanical view of scientific explanation. On such a view, the whole is conceived of as the product of the parts by their mutual interaction. Today, such a view would imply that atoms are the product of mutual interaction among electrons, protons, and neutrons, for example, and molecules are the product of mutual interaction among atoms. Compounds are the product of interaction among molecules, and so on. This is the "building-block" view of the universe, and though the details have changed over time it is a view as old as the atomists of the 5th century BC.

Aristotle did not hold back on his repudiation of atomism. In their attempt to lay out a purely material and mechanical explanation of natural phenomena, atomists strike Aristotle as "drunken stutterers." Aristotle found it preposterous to suggest that the characteristic problems of biology, for example, could be solved by means of mechanical categories alone, without the addition of teleological explanations. While he recognizes that material causes are a necessary part of an adequate explanation, a phenomenon such as phototropism in plants, for example, could never be adequately explained, according to Aristotle, without reference to that for the sake of which they move towards light.

Aristotle also regards Empedocles (5th century BC) as utterly mistaken in his theory of the origin of species, according to which nature (matter in motion) produces every possible type of animal (e.g., cattle with human faces) over time, though only those forms that are coherently and consistently constructed survive. Instead, Aristotle contends that nature is a cause which acts not blindly, but purposively. An adequate explanation of organic phenomena, including the origin of species, must include, in addition to an account of matter and motion, the ends towards which functional organic activity is directed. Again, Aristotle regards material and efficient causes as necessary conditions for an adequate explanation of natural phenomena. They are insufficient, however, without the addition of final causality.

It is important to emphasize that, whereas Plato held an *exclusively* teleological view of nature, disparaging mechanistic materialism, and the atomists held an exclusively materialist mechanistic view, Aristotle argues that a comprehensive account of nature must include both. Indeed, he makes substantial contributions to the concepts of material and mechanical causes. This is important in order to remedy the mischaracterization of Aristotle as promulgating exclusively teleological explanation of nature, as Plato does. Teleology and material mechanics are both at work in nature, according to Aristotle; especially in organic nature.

One reason for the mischaracterization of Aristotle is the use to which his ideas were put in the medieval period. Aristotelian teleology dominated both Christian and Muslim thought throughout the middle ages. With a conception of God as the intelligent cause by which all natural objects are ordered to an end, mechanical explanations were regarded as superfluous, if not heretical. Natural philosophy, the science of the day, was entirely at the service of theology. Modern science rejected this view of course, in large part by rejecting Aristotelian teleology. But it was a defective form of Aristotelian teleology that modern science cast off. For, Aristotle would have rejected the medieval notion of exclusively teleological explanations of nature, as he rejected Plato's teleology. Again, Aristotle demands teleology in conjunction with material and mechanical causes.

Francis Bacon (1561-1626), a contemporary of Galileo Galilei (1564-1642) and Johannes Kepler (1571-1630), is the philosopher of the modern scientific revolution. He sets the stage for modern philosophy by arguing that the works of Plato and Aristotle are inferior to the physicalistic philosophies of their predecessors such as the ancient atomists. Furthermore, according to Bacon, modern philosophy should be restricted to the investigation of nature, which is to say that the only valuable philosophy is natural philosophy (i.e., science). Bacon's view is precisely that philosophy is properly epistemology, and epistemology is knowledge of the sciences.

Bacon lays out certain "idols of the tribe" which he thinks must be rejected in a suitable investigation of nature. Among them is explanation, or, more accurately, interpretation, in terms of final causes. Final causes in physics, he contends, are like Vestal virgins, beautiful but sterile keepers of the fire. Therefore, Bacon consigns final causes to metaphysics and religion, wherein we might marvel at what God "intends" at a safe distance from serious science.

Aristotle's scientific limitations, especially with respect to the motion of the heavenly bodies, made matters worse for teleology in the modern scientific revolution. Astrological discoveries by Kepler and Galileo made Aristotle's notion of celestial orbs moving towards ends ridiculous. Add in the legacy of medieval neo-Aristotelian teleology devoid of explanation of natural phenomena in terms of matter and motion, and modern science and philosophy leave teleology behind. To close the deal, modern philosophers such as Descartes (1596-1650) and Spinoza (1632-1677) presented philosophical arguments for the rejection of final causes, claiming that efficient causes are necessary and sufficient for an account of the natural world.

At the same time, however, Isaac Newton (1642-1727) developed a mathematical approach to scientific explanation that shifted away from causal explanations altogether. Instead, Newtonian science is purely descriptive. For instance, Newton offers no account of the *cause* of gravitation. Instead, he identifies the phenomena of gravity (observation) and describes those phenomena with mathematical precision. When Newton's laws of motion are used in conjunction with causal concepts, as they are when the laws are applied and the data is interpreted, such accounts are in terms of efficient causes only. Thus, a force applied to a mass, for example, is conceived of as the efficient cause of a given acceleration.

The Newtonian method of pure description plus mathematical precision is the model behind the logical positivists' view that all knowledge comprises observation statements (descriptions) and statements that are reducible to observation statements by logical and mathematical reasoning. It is the idea at work in the view that descriptive statements are logically distinct from normative statements, and that knowledge pertains exclusively to the logical space of descriptions.

(I argue in Chapter Five that, while we must affirm the dichotomy of logical spaces and preserve pure natural-scientific description, knowledge does not belong to the logical space of pure descriptions. Instead, 'knowledge' entails reasons, and the logical space of reasons is not the space of pure descriptions. It is, rather, a *normative* space. It is precisely for this reason that value and knowledge, including natural-scientific knowledge, are not separable, and why, in the broadest sense, epistemology and ethics are not logically distinct.)

Teleology is essential to the natural law theory of ethics. It plays a central role in Aquinas' development of natural law. Such theories conceive of goods as *that for the sake of which* actions are performed or intended. A final good, then, is that which is sought for its own sake and not for the sake of something else, with all other things ultimately sought for the sake of it. The basic idea behind natural law is that basic goods are derived from the natural ends towards which human beings are directed. These are thought to include such goods as life, health, friendship, etc., with happiness as the final good.

As we have seen, however, Hume disparages natural law theories of ethics by arguing that prescriptive "ought" statements cannot be derived from descriptive "is" statements. Even if it is true that human beings do act towards natural ends, it does not follow that they ought to do so. According to Hume, there is a logical gap between description and prescription. At the same time, modern science abandoned teleology to pursue pure descriptions which cash out in terms of efficient causes only. The result of these two developments in modern thought is, as we have seen, the separation of ethics and epistemology.

PHILOSOPHY OF MATHEMATICS

Hume's purported fact/value gap and the modern scientific rejection of teleology drove a wedge between knowledge and morality. Developments in the philosophy of mathematics further exacerbated the dichotomization of ethics and epistemology in early analytic philosophy. This section charts some of those developments.

Twentieth century epistemology in both the analytic and continental traditions traces back to a reaction against logical psychologism—a 19th century movement that sought to ground logical and mathematical laws on psychological facts. Logical psychologism enjoyed prestige among thoroughgoing empiricists, such as John Stuart Mill (1806-1873) who sought to account for all human knowledge on the basis of sensory experience alone. On this view, psychology is the experimental study of regularities governing mental phenomena, and mental phenomena are reducible to two classes: sense-impressions and mental images formed from earlier sense impressions. Logic and mathematics, on this view, are nothing more than manipulations of mental images or ideas ultimately derived from sense-impressions; for instance, seeing that two apples added to two more already in the bag yields four apples.

Frege criticizes the views of logical psychologism in his *Foundations of Arithmetic*, while Husserl independently develops a sustained refutation of psychologism and by extension empiricism in the first volume of his *Logical Investigations*. But it is the different methodologies the two philosophers developed in their reactions against psychologism that defines the distinction between analytic epistemology and phenomenology in the twentieth century.

Against the prevailing empiricism of his day and its attendant mind/world dualism (physical facts about objects such as apples impress the senses and are separated into various mental facts), Husserl's phenomenology sought the justification of cognition not in the techniques of modern natural science and technology, but in the reflective, evidential, descriptive awareness of a simultaneity of the structures and objects of consciousness, of modes of

48 Daniel P. Haggerty

awareness and objects of awareness. That is, Husserl's phenomenology grounds justification of cognition on descriptive awareness of phenomena disclosed to consciousness. In *Philosophy as Rigorous Science*, Husserl writes:

> How can experience as consciousness give or contact an object? How can experiences be mutually legitimated or corrected by means of each other, and not merely replace each other or confirm each other subjectively? How can the play of consciousness whose logic is empirical make objectively valid statements, valid for things that are in and for themselves? Why are the playing rules, so to speak, of consciousness not irrelevant for things? How is natural science to be comprehensible in absolutely every case, to the extent that it pretends at every step to posit and to know a nature that is in itself—in itself in opposition to the subjective flow of consciousness? All these questions become riddles as soon as reflection on them becomes serious. It is well known that theory of knowledge is the discipline that wants to answer such questions, and also that up to the present, despite all the thoughtfulness employed by the greatest scholars in regard to those questions, this discipline (epistemology) has not answered in a manner scientifically clear, unanimous, and decisive.[4]

and then:

> It is then clear: there is, properly speaking, only one nature, the one that appears in the appearances of things.[5]

In *Ideas Pertaining to a Pure Phenomenology*, Husserl develops these ideas further. He writes:

> The world is the sum-total of objects of possible experience and experiential cognition, of objects that, on the basis of actual experiences, are cognizable in correct theoretical thinking.[6]

Thus, regarding phenomenological epistemology:

---

[4] Edmund Husserl, "Philosophy as Rigorous Science," translated in Q. Lauer (ed.), *Phenomenology and the Crisis of Philosophy* (New York: Harper, 1965), 88.

[5] Husserl, "Philosophy as Rigorous Science," 106.

[6] Edmund Husserl, *Ideas Pertaining to a Pure Phenomenology and to a Phenomenological Philosophy—First Book: General Introduction to a Pure Phenomenology*, translated by F. Kersten (The Hague: Nijhoff, 1982), 6.

That the "essences" grasped by essential intuition permit, at least to a very great extent, of being fixed in definitive concepts and thereby afford possibilities of definitive and in their own way absolutely valid objective statements, is evident to anyone free of prejudice.[7]

Phenomenology is the study of the structures of consciousness as they are experienced from the first-person perspective. Husserl employs phenomenology as a refutation of logical psychologism. The structure of experience is, as Husserl argues, always experience of some object. This implies that the subject/object dichotomy that is presupposed not only by logical psychologism but also more broadly by the empiricism of modern epistemology, the dichotomy of knowing subject on one side and knowable object on the other, is disconfirmed phenomenologically. Husserl's phenomenology is later developed and significantly modified by Heidegger, Sartre, and Merleau-Ponty. Still, it remains influential in twentieth century continental epistemology.

Like phenomenology, Anglo-American epistemology in the early part of the twentieth century develops in response to problems for empiricism, the view that all knowledge is observational. In particular, problems with the empiricism of early twentieth century Anglo-American philosophers such as Russell, Carnap, and Ayer gave rise to the development of analytic epistemology. However in order to understand the different method with which problems for empiricism were handled in the analytic tradition, as opposed to the method of phenomenology, it is first important to see how Frege's reaction against logical psychologism differs from Husserl's.

In *The Foundations of Arithmetic*, Frege writes:

...sensations are absolutely no concern of arithmetic. No more are mental pictures, formed from the amalgamated traces of earlier sense-impressions. All these phases of consciousness are characteristically fluctuating and indefinite, in strong contrast to the definiteness and fixity of the concepts of objects of mathematics... Psychology should not imagine that it can contribute anything whatever to the foundation of arithmetic... Never, then, let us suppose that the essence of the matter lies in such ideas. Never let us take a description of the origin of an idea for a definition, or an account of the mental and physical conditions on which we become conscious of a

---

[7] Husserl, "Philosophy as Rigorous Science," 111.

proposition for proof of it. A proposition may be thought, and again it may be true; let us never confuse these two things.[8]

In his refutation of psychologism, Frege draws an important distinction between concepts and ideas. Ideas are the mental images which are the subject matter of the psychology of his day. Concepts, on the other hand, are an object of study for the analyst and mathematician. Unlike ideas, they neither fluctuate nor develop; rather, we discover and express them. As Frege argues, the concept C identifies what is distinctive about C—what separates C from everything else. The idea of two apples added to two more already in the bag is not in any way an adequate account of the concept four. The fluctuating and idiosyncratic mental images people associate with C (apples, bags) are not what separate C from everything else. Whatever images a person might have in association with the number 3, for example, or with the number 777864, those images do not fix the meaning of the concepts expressed by those numbers.

As Frege explains, "A definition of a concept … must be complete; it must unambiguously determine, as regards any object, whether or not it falls under the concept…"[9] Thus, the definition of the concept 'prime' must map not only every number to a truth-value, but every non-numerical object as well (e.g., the Moon). The definition must map whether the following statements, and innumerable others, are true or false: 1 is prime, 2 is prime, 3 is prime, 4 is prime, the Moon is prime, etc. Otherwise, the definition fails to specify a sharp boundary and consequently fails to specify a concept. "To a concept without sharp boundary there would correspond an area that…faded away into the background. This would not really be an area at all; and likewise a concept that is not sharply defined is wrongly termed a concept."[10] From these remarks, we can see Frege as the progenitor of analytic epistemology and the originator of a most austere, rigorous conceptual analysis as philosophical methodology.

We can go farther, however, towards understanding the split between continental and analytic methodology generally, and epistemology in particular. For one, like Frege, Husserl and all phenomenology rejects positing mental images or representations as objects of knowledge. For, the

---

[8] Gottlob Frege, *The Foundations of Arithmetic*, translated by J. L. Austin (Evanston, Illinois: Northwestern University Press, 1986), VI.

[9] Peter Geach and Max Black, *Translations from the Philosophical Writings of Gottlob Frege* (Oxford: Basil Blackwell, 1985), 139.

[10] Ibid.

phenomenological theory of intentionality claims that consciousness is always *consciousness of*.... That is, consciousness is always "out there" beyond itself with whatever entities towards which it is directed. Thus, the notion that ideas are objects of knowledge is rejected by both phenomenological and analytic epistemology. The real crux of the difference between phenomenology and Fregean conceptual analysis—at least as it is seen looking back from the perspective of analytic philosophy developed in the twentieth century—traces back to Frege's and Husserl's different responses to the so-called Paradox of Analysis (also known as the Learner's Paradox).

In the broadest sense, analysis can be defined as the mode of explanation that works back to what is more fundamental by breaking down what is to be analyzed into its constituent parts. Analysis of the concept 'knowledge', for example, involves identifying the various concepts constitutive of the concept 'knowledge', including the concepts of 'truth', 'justification', and 'belief'. These more basic concepts are then broken down into their constitutive parts, which is to say the conditions for their application, which identifies their boundaries and separates them from everything else. Once sorted out in this way, an attempt is made to identify the relations between the various elementary concepts.

Now the *paradox* of analysis is first raised in Plato's *Meno*. The paradox seems to imply that all conceptual analysis is either pointless or incorrect. It is pointless if with the concept being analyzed one already thinks everything contained in the analysis. If truth, belief, and justification, for example, are already contained in the concept knowledge, if with the concept knowledge we already think "justified true belief," then analysis would seem to be of no benefit. On the other hand, if analysis is not pointless then its results are inadequate. For, if the result of conceptual analysis is a sense or meaning different from the meaning of the original concept to be analyzed, then the analyzan and analyzandum are not logically equivalent.[11] This paradox was of great importance to Plato. His efforts to resolve the paradox formed the foundations of *apriorism* and transcendental idealism.

Husserl faces the paradox and, early on, comes to the conclusion that it is irresolvable, and that hence fruitful analysis is impossible. In place of analysis, Husserl went on, as we have seen, to develop an account of the general structure of thought, including an account of the structure of mathematical

---

[11] For a fuller account of Frege and Husserl on the Paradox of Analysis see Michael Dummett, *Frege and Other Philosophers* (Oxford: Oxford University Press, 1996). I am much indebted to Dummett's excellent book throughout this section.

52 Daniel P. Haggerty

thought. Frege, on the other hand, rejects—that is, *resolves*—the paradox. In so doing he develops important contributions to the philosophy of language and an understanding of the nature of thoughts and their inner structure.

The distinction between sense and reference is at the heart of how Frege resolves the Learner's Paradox. Mathematicians, for example, are ultimately concerned not with the sense of words, or the ideas associated with them. Instead, they are concerned "with the matter itself," which is to say the *referents* of mathematical concepts.[12] Mathematical definitions may employ different senses and give rise to different ideas without becoming *incorrect* on that count. So long as they have the same reference the relation between the concepts employed corresponds to the identity relation between objects. Analysis, then, is genuinely informative by revealing different senses of the same referent. The analyzan and analyzandum are logically equivalent, they assert the identity relation; yet the analysis is genuinely informative insofar as it reveals different senses of that to which the terms refer. For instance, the concept '27+19' and the concept '46' have the same referent but different senses. The proposition "27+19=46" is genuinely informative (not pointless) because it asserts that the two different senses are related to the same referent by the identity relation. It is in this way that mathematics is both logically necessary and genuinely informative—and not psychologistic.

Thus, while both Husserl and Frege were concerned with epistemology stimulated by their interest in understanding the nature of thought, Husserl's phenomenological epistemology proceeds from the descriptive awareness of phenomena disclosed to consciousness. Analytic epistemology, by contrast, proceeds from conceptual analysis to the identification and greater clarification of that to which our concepts, or the linguistic items used to express them, refer. As Michael Dummett explains:

> Frege and Husserl were obviously right to hold (against the empiricists of their day) that perception is not simply a matter of sensation, but that it has a further component at least analogous to thought. Frege simply identified it with thought, whereas Husserl wanted it to be a generalization of thought; but the one failed to show how thought could be fused with sensation, while the other failed to explain how the notion of thought was capable of generalization.

and,

---

[12] Dummett, 125.

> Husserl was the founder of phenomenology, Frege the grandfather of analytic philosophy, two schools which today are generally regarded as utterly diverse and barely capable of communicating with one another... (Yet) just after the publication of (Husserl's *Logische Untersuchungen*), Frege and Husserl would have appeared...remarkably close in their philosophical views: what was it in the thought of each that set their followers on such divergent paths? Frege was the first philosopher in history to achieve anything resembling a plausible account of the nature of thoughts and of their inner structure. His account depended upon his conviction of the parallelism between thought and language. His interest was in thought, not in language for its own sake... Nevertheless, his strategy for analysing thought was to analyse the forms of its linguistic or symbolic expression; and this strategy became the characteristic mark of the analytical school.[13]

This brief account is intended only to paint in the broadest strokes a picture of the origins of the analytic/continental split, as understood from the perspective of analytic philosophers generally, and Dummett in particular. To be sure, Dummett's interpretation of Husserl is quite selective. But the main point for present purposes is to understand how early analytic epistemology understood itself, and partly in contradistinction from how it understood phenomenology.

IMPLICATIONS FOR EPISTEMOLOGY

Ultimately, though the work of Hume and modern science are also central, the deepest split between ethics and epistemology is the result of early twentieth century analytic philosophy more than anything else. From *this* perspective, the split seems to begin with the analytic appropriation of Hume and to end, rightly, in logical empiricism (also known as logical positivism).

Logical positivism grew out of the Vienna Circle in the nineteen twenties with the work of philosophers such as Rudolph Carnap, Otto Neurath, Moritz Schlick, and others. Members of the Circle originally met to discuss philosophy of science and epistemology. Their views were shaped by two primary influences. One was their interpretation of Hume on the status of matters of fact in science and the relations between ideas in logic and mathematics. Regarding these as the only adequate generators of true propositions, they decried the comparatively poor epistemic status of religion

---

[13] Dummett, 286-287.

and ethics. The second major influence was their reading of Frege on the value of analyticity and the importance of linguistic meaning. Based on these two doctrines, the Circle produced a manifesto endorsing logical positivism (also known as logical empiricism). Logical positivism combines the claim that the only authentic knowledge is scientific knowledge with a version of *apriorism*—the idea that propositional knowledge can be derived analytically. That is, all knowledge is produced either from experience or from logical analysis. An important upshot of this is what became known as the logical empiricists' Verificationist Principle of Meaning. According to this principle, only statements in science, logic, and mathematics have a definite cognitive meaning. Thus statements in metaphysics, ethics, and religion are literally meaningless. More than two thousand years of effort in these endeavors has produced only nonsense. Accordingly, there is no place for the language of ethics and metaphysics in epistemology.

(It is worth noting that the Verificationist Principle of Meaning continued to be employed even after it was noted that the principle itself cannot be verified by science, logic, or mathematics! Indeed, vestiges of verificationism remain today in the attitude that only science and mathematics produce propositions that are true.)

Things began to change with the publication of Gilbert Ryle's, *The Concept of Mind* (1949). Ryle's watershed book is a work in the philosophy of mind using the techniques of analytic philosophy, which is to say logical and linguistic analysis. Ryle develops a behaviorist account of mind/body language in order to overcome the "Cartesian Myth"—that is, Descartes' conception of the mind as an immaterial entity ontologically distinct from but governing the body. Instead, Ryle argues that the function of mind-body language is to describe or explain from the evidence of their behavior how higher-order organisms like humans exhibit evidence of consciousness. Such "mental" vocabulary, or a vocabulary of consciousness, Ryle argues, is a perfectly legitimate way of explaining human behavior empirically.

According to Ryle, philosophical pseudo-problems like Descartes' difficulty in account for how an immaterial mind interacts causally with a material body arise only when philosophers attempt to attribute observable behavioral qualities to an ontologically separate realm of mind, soul, or consciousness. Metaphysical mind-body dualism is explanatorily superfluous, Ryle argues, and a monistic view of mind in terms of the empirically observable properties of organisms is advanced. For present purposes, however, the most important upshot of Ryle's work is that it does indeed have metaphysical consequences, namely, monism with respect to mind and body.

Contrary to the claims of the logical empiricists, Ryle's work seemed to show that logical and conceptual analysis could produce metaphysical results that were not cognitively meaningless. His book is precisely a solution to the metaphysical mind/body problem, yet it is in line with the Fregean method of conceptual analysis.

Ryle's work informed much of analytic epistemology in the second half of the twentieth century. Following his analysis of 'mind', epistemologists treated 'belief' and 'knowledge' not as occurent introspectible mental states, not as empirically inaccessible first-person states of consciousness, but rather as *dispositions to behave* in such and such ways. Following Frege, since mental states and ideas fluctuate and develop, they cannot be the objects of knowledge. Understanding knowledge, then, is not a matter of investigating ideas or mental states, but a matter of analyzing the concept 'knowledge'. Certainly belief is an important component of knowledge, but the concept 'belief' may be outsourced to philosophy of mind or philosophy of psychology for thoroughgoing analysis. For purposes of epistemology, a dispositional analysis in terms of a propensity to behave in certain specifiable ways under certain specifiable conditions is an adequate treatment of the concept 'belief'. To say, for example, that Jones *believes* that it is raining is to say that he is disposed to reach for his umbrella.

In this way, analytic epistemology renders mental concepts associated with knowledge intelligible not by intuition or phenomenological description, but by conceptual analysis. Analysis of the concept K (knowledge) identifies what is distinctive about K—what separates K from everything else, such as false beliefs and lucky guesses. In this way analysis is thought to determine unambiguously what precisely does and does not fall under the scope of a given concept. Analysis of 'knowledge' and other epistemic concepts determine the boundaries of knowledge by determining the conditions for the application of the terms and the concepts they express. This is the framework and the methodology with which half a century of work is carried out in analytic epistemology.

In "Problems and Changes in the Empiricist Criterion of Meaning" (1950), Carl Hempel identifies the epistemology of modern empiricism with the view that all non-analytic knowledge is based on experience. His article investigates the logical empiricists' claim that a sentence has cognitive meaning (that is, is true or false) only if it is either analytic (true by definition) or capable of experiential verification. Hempel's arguments, which fit nicely with Ryle's, proceed by analysis of such concepts as 'verification', 'testability', and 'falsifiability'. The result is the demise of the idea that the only things that can be known, the only statements that have cognitive meaning, are those that are ultimately empirically verifiable observation statements. Whereas Ryle revives metaphysics via conceptual analysis—and recall that metaphysics had been included with ethics and religion in the set of things about which it was supposed that we cannot speak meaningfully— Hempel shows, via analysis, that knowledge is not reducible to observation statements.

> Hence, what is sweepingly referred to as "the (cognitive) meaning" of a given scientific hypothesis cannot be adequately characterized in terms of potential observational evidence alone, nor can it be specified for the hypothesis taken in isolation: In order to understand "the meaning" of a hypothesis within an empiricist language, we have to know not merely what observation sentences it entails alone or in conjunction with subsidiary hypotheses, but also what other, non-observational, empirical sentences are entailed by it, what sentences in the given language would confirm or disconfirm it, and for what other hypotheses the given one would be confirmatory or disconfirmatory. In other words, the cognitive meaning of a statement in an empiricist language is reflected in the totality of its logical relationships to all other statements in tat language and not to the observation sentences alone. In this sense, the statements of empirical science have a surplus meaning over and above what can be expressed in terms of relevant observation sentences.[14]

According to the Verificationist Principle non-observational statements such as "The contents are radioactive" are either meaningless (which is obviously false), or else they are meaningful because they are reducible to direct observation statements. What Hempel shows is that no such reduction can be carried off. Instead, such statements, like so many assertions in empirical science, make sense only in reference to an array of other statements in an empiricist language. Therefore, Hempel argues that we should understand cognitive meaningfulness as *translatability into an empiricist language*. The cognitive meaning of a sentence, then, is reflected not in its logical relation to observation statements, but in its relation to all other statements in an empiricist language.

In "Two Dogmas of Empiricism" (1951), W. V. O. Quine takes Hempel's conclusions further. Quine argues that modern empiricism, including logical

---

[14] Carl Hempel, Problems and Changes in the Empiricist Criterion of Meaning. *Revue Internationale de Philosophie*, (1950) 11: 59.

empiricism, rests on two dogmas: (1) a distinction between analytic and synthetic propositions, and (2) reductionism. The analytic-synthetic distinction goes back to Kant, who distinguishes propositions that are true simply by virtue of their meaning (analytic) from propositions that are not (synthetic). Logical empiricists take up Kant's distinction and argue that synthetic truths are knowable based on empirical verification while mathematical and logical truths are analytic, knowable by the meanings of terms and the conventions of language. Synthetic truths, such as "The normal boiling point of water is 99.97 degrees Celsius at 101.325 kPa" are supposedly grounded on matters of fact. Analytic truths, such as "All bachelors are unmarried men" are supposedly based on meaning independently of matters of fact. And all meaningful statements, according to logical empiricism, are either synthetic or analytic.

Quine presents a thoroughgoing analysis of the concept 'analyticity' and argues that all putative definitions of the concept have serious shortcomings. If we cannot fix the meaning of the concept 'analyticity' then it makes no sense to claim that all meaningful propositions are either synthetic or analytic, which is to say that logical empiricism is based on a distinction the meaning of which cannot be fixed. Moreover, Quine shows that reductionism is bound up with the purported analytic/synthetic distinction, and so this dogma of empiricism must also be abandoned. As an alternative to reductionism and logical empiricism, Quine proposes that "our statements about the external world face the tribunal of sense experience not individually but only as a corporate body."[15] Quine's arguments on these matters have had two important and lasting effects on Anglo-American philosophy.

First, together with Hempel, Quine brings an end to logical empiricism specifically, and to modern empiricism generally—to the view, based on a reading of Hume, that genuine knowledge is restricted to descriptive statements (observation statements) plus mathematical and logical constructs (analyticity). Instead, Quine endorses a pragmatic empiricism that is line with American Pragmatists William James (1842-1910) and John Dewey (1859-1952).

In "A World of Pure Experience," James sought to overcome the deficiencies of modern empiricism which placed explanatory emphasis on parts of experience (a sensory datum, immediate experience, reductionism), and regarded the whole of experience as a collection of parts. In this way,

---

[15] Quoted in Paul Moser and Arnold vander Nat, *Human Knowledge* (Oxford: Oxford University Press, 1987), 224. In this section I am indebted to Moser and vander Nat's lengthy, informative introduction.

58 Daniel P. Haggerty

James argues, modern empiricism is atomistic, over-emphasizing the disjunction between parts. James calls instead for a "radical empiricism" that treats the conjunctive as experienced. This anticipates Quine's notion of facing the tribunal of experience as a corporate body. We do not face a sensory datum or an observation statement one at a time, building knowledge up from the smallest parts of experience. Instead, our propositions face the world of experience and the language of empiricism holistically, and receive their confirmation or disconfirmation from the whole.

Further, in "Pragmatism's Conception of Truth," James defines truth as an important kind of activity, namely as one which works in the way of belief. He explains, "True ideas lead us into useful verbal and conceptual quarters as well as directly up to useful sensible termini. They lead to consistency, stability and flowing human intercourse... all true processes must lead to the face of directly verifying sensible experiences somewhere"[16] And in "What Pragmatism Means," James argues that the central point of pragmatism is that,

> ...truth is one species of good, and not, as is usually supposed, a category distinct from good, and coordinate with it. Truth is the name of whatever proves itself to be good in the way of belief, and good, too, for definite, assignable reasons.[17]

If truth is what is good in the way of belief, Hume's is/ought distinction is misconceived. For descriptive statements about what is the case do imply what ought to be believed.

Such pragmatic conceptions of experience and truth connect to the second important and lasting effect of Quine's "Two Dogmas of Empiricism" in Anglo-American philosophy. Namely, a break-down in the distinction between empirical science and speculative metaphysics—a distinction that early analysts saw as sacrosanct, growing out of the Enlightenment and reaching fulfillment in logical empiricism. Today, analytic philosophy is very much occupied with metaphysics. Four-dimensionalism, for example, is contemporary theory of ontology which argues that material objects have temporal parts as well as spatial parts. Four-dimensionalism and other contemporary analytic metaphysics is closely connected to science, and is

---

[16] William James, Pragmatism's Conception of Truth. Lecture 6 (1907) in *Pragmatism: A new name for some old ways of thinking* (New York: Hackett, 1981), 100.

[17] Also in *Pragmatism: A new name for some old ways of thinking* (New York: Hackett, 1981), 37.

sometimes described as philosophy of science. The aim of analytic metaphysics is not a mere description of our conceptual scheme, our way of organizing experiential content that is susceptible to conceptual organization. The aim is, rather, the truth about what there is, about what the world is really like.

In his 2002 acclaimed *Four Dimensionalism: An Ontology of Persistent and Time*, Theodore Sider explains, "I want to (give an account of) what kinds of things the material world contains and how they are related, and this at a very high level of abstraction, focusing on issues of parthood, time, and persistence."[18] And, "Science is certainly relevant to metaphysics since inconsistency with a firmly established scientific theory is as good a reason against a theory as one could ask for. But science invariably leaves many questions open. One of these, I think, is whether things have temporal parts."[19] Sider then lays out his methodology, showing how analytic metaphysics supplements science, in contrast to the earlier views of logical empiricism, which, growing out of the Enlightenment, condemned metaphysics as meaningless:

> I...proceed assuming that reasonable belief in metaphysics is indeed possible, and that something like the following methodology is legitimate. One approaches inquiry with a number of beliefs. Many of these will not trace back to empirical beliefs, at least not in any direct way. These beliefs may be particular, as for the example that I was once a young boy, or they may be more general and theoretical, for example the belief that identity is transitive. One then develops a theory preserving as many of these ordinary beliefs as possible, while remaining consistent with science. There is a familiar give and take: one must be prepared to sacrifice some beliefs one initially held in order to develop a satisfying theoretical account. But a theoretical account should take ordinary belief as a whole seriously, for only ordinary beliefs tie down inquiry.[20]

To sum up this chapter, ethics, along with metaphysics, had been completely sheared away from epistemology in early twentieth century analytic philosophy. Through their reading of Hume and Frege, early analysts viewed knowledge as exclusively scientific, while ethics and metaphysics were regarded as literally meaningless. The work of Ryle, Hempel, and Quine, among others, helped to change that. It did so not by disparaging science, nor

---

[18] Theodore Sider, *Four-Dimensionalism* (Oxford: Oxford University Press, 2001), xiv.
[19] Ibid.
[20] *Four-Dimensionalism*, xv-xvi.

by turning away from empiricism. Rather, conceptual analysis showed that empiricism itself cannot be adequately conceived of atomistically, and that cognitive meaningfulness cannot be conceived of in terms of reducibility to observation statements. Mental states, episodes, or dispositions, including belief and knowledge, were amenable to analysis. Even metaphysics can be conducted in concert with empirical language and make meaningful contributions to knowledge. Quine's notion of the *tribunal* of experience, echoing James' notion that truth is one species of *good*, made room once more for normativity in epistemology.

The next chapter investigates developments in analytic epistemology in the second half of the twentieth century, wherein *epistemic justification* is the primary evaluative concept. These developments lead to the reunion of epistemology and ethics around the concept *virtue*.

Chapter 4

VIRTUE EPISTEMOLOGY: FROM (JTB) TO (VE)

THE (JTB) MODEL OF KNOWLEDGE

This chapter maps the development of analytic epistemology in the second half of the twentieth century. It shows how debate over the meaning and structure of epistemic justification produced recent inquiry into the notion of intellectual virtue.

That knowledge is true justified belief is a twentieth century idea. It is sometimes claimed that this is the definition of knowledge that Plato formulates in *Meno* and *Theaetetus*. That is not quite right, however. While Plato does show that true belief is not sufficient for knowledge, he never proposes justification as a third condition. Instead, Plato suggests that in addition to having true belief, a knower must be able to provide an account or explain why the true belief is true.

In the modern era, Descartes (1596-1650) and Locke (1632-1704) regarded knowledge as a psychological state, and one that is different from belief. They reasoned that while truth and falsity apply to belief, they do not apply to knowledge. That is, though it is intelligible to think or say that what Smith *believes* is false, it makes no sense to say that what Smith *knows* is false. Hence they define knowledge as self-guaranteeing certainty of what is immediately recognizable in present awareness. A belief, they argue, is a psychological state whose propositional content may or may not correspond to reality.

By the middle of the twentieth century, however, the modern intuitive notion that knowledge is immediate awareness of facts had been abandoned, and for good reasons. Following Frege, Wittgenstein, and Ryle, the modern philosophical account of knowledge gets the grammar of "knowledge" wrong by taking it to be an occurrent mental act or state—an immediate recognition of present awareness. The problem with this account is that claims of introspective certainty cannot be observed, or analyzed conceptually. Moreover, what seems introspectively certain may be patently false. Instead, meaningful investigation about the difference between knowledge and belief must regard both 'knowledge' and 'belief' as dispositions to behave, rather than as private mental phenomena.

Belief is necessary for knowledge. It makes no sense to say that a subject knows something but does not believe it. (Not wanting to believe what one knows is another matter.) The idea that someone can know something without believing it results from confusing knowing with knowing that one knows. We can and do know things without believing that we know, and therefore without knowing that we know, but this is not the same as knowing without believing. An example may help. When driving a familiar route, we know where to turn. If we know to turn at the third traffic light, say, then we believe that is where we should turn—that we believe it is evidenced in our turning there. Yet we may not *believe that we know* to turn at the third light, having no belief about the matter one way or another. Such a situation may be revealed when we are asked to give directions. We know to turn at the third light; we do it almost every day. Yet we may not know that we know it, in which case we are at a loss about how to give directions. Further, if knowing something required believing that we know, then in order to know that we believe that we know, we would have to believe *that*, and so on. If this were the case, then knowing one thing would require an infinite regress of beliefs, which is absurd.

Though necessary, belief is not sufficient for knowledge. This is obvious insofar as some beliefs are false. Therefore, *true* belief is necessary for knowledge. Both conditions, truth and belief, must be met. Is true belief sufficient for knowledge? Are all cases of true belief knowledge, and are all cases of knowledge true belief? Nearly all contemporary epistemologists agree that true belief is not sufficient—that it is not an adequate analysis of the concept 'knowledge'. The reason for this is that it is possible for the truth condition to be related to belief only accidently, or by luck. For instance, if a man spends all of his earnings on lottery tickets because, as he says, he "knows" he will win and he wins, we do not say that he did in fact know, and that his behavior was warranted. We say, rather, that he got lucky—or that it was a remarkable coincidence. Even if he believed that he would win, and, as it turns out, his belief was true, he did not know. For reasons like these contemporary epistemologists hold that a third condition, *justification*, is necessary to guarantee that the truth condition is not related to the belief condition accidentally. This gives us a tripartite theory of knowledge. The conceptual meaning of sentences of the type "S knows that p" is given in the set of individually necessary and jointly sufficient conditions: (1) S believes that p; (2) p is true; and (3) the belief that p (or S's believing P) is justified.

Edmund Gettier established the tripartite theory as the object of analysis in epistemology with an article he in 1963, "Is Justified True Belief Knowledge?" Ironically, Gettier's article is in fact a challenge to the tripartite view, insofar as he argues that justified true belief (JTB) may not be sufficient for knowledge. Still, Gettier's succinct argument generated so much response over the next several decades, including several attempts to save (JTB), that it set (JTB) as the model for analysis even while Gettier himself seems to regard it as inadequate.

Gettier argues that there are cases involving beliefs that are both true and justified, but which appear not to be cases in which genuine knowledge can be claimed. Gettier's first counterexample is sufficient to make the general point. Imagine that Smith interviews for a job and forms the justified belief that "Jones will get the job," perhaps because he overheard it said by a credible source that Jones would get the offer. Imagine further that Smith also has a justified true belief that "Jones has ten coins in his pocket," perhaps having observed Jones empty out his pocket and count the coins. On the basis of these two justified beliefs Smith deduces by transitivity the justified belief that, "The man who will get the job has ten coins in his pocket." As it turns out, however, Smith gets the job and happens to have ten coins in his pocket. So his belief "The man who will get the job has ten coins in his pocket" is justified and true, but not a case of knowledge. On the basis of this example and another like it, Gettier concludes that (JTB) is an inadequate definition of the concept 'knowledge'. Further analysis is needed to uncover what exactly the concept 'knowledge' means.

For the first twenty years after the publication of Gettier's article, epistemologists attempted to handle the Gettier problem in one of two ways. Either show that (JTB) is correct under closer analysis of the concept 'justification' and that Gettier's examples are not genuine counterexamples, or else accept Gettier's conclusion and attempt to formulate a fourth condition for knowledge. Even today, many epistemologists accept that knowledge is (JTB) plus whatever solves the Gettier problem and rules out cases of accidental justified true belief. The result has been almost half a century of very careful analysis of the concept 'epistemic justification'—the very concept and analysis which, as we shall see, ultimately leads epistemology back to the concept 'virtue'.

One early response to Gettier, however, did attempt to bypass the (JTB) model and with it the notion of epistemic justification. Alvin Goldman (1967) and Marshall Swain (1972) each proposed causal theories of knowledge. The general idea is that "S knows that p"—that is, a subject S knows that some propositions p is true—if and only if the fact that p is causally connected with S's believing that p, and S correctly reconstructs important links in the relevant causal chain. The problem with causal theories, however, is that they are too weak for knowledge. S may be fully warranted in believing that the causal connection between the belief that p and the fact that p obtains, and it does obtain, but S's background evidence may consists of a badly biased sample, such that S could not be said to 'know' that p. In such cases, S would meet the conditions of a causal theory and yet not know. Indeed, Goldman subsequently acknowledged problems with his causal theory and went on to develop versions of justification in terms of reliabilism instead.

The literature on 'epistemic justification' after Gettier is vast. One of the foremost contributors to the field is Roderick Chisholm. In "Knowledge as Justified True belief" (1982), Chisholm aims to defend the (JTB) account of knowledge against Gettier-style counterexamples. Roughly, Chisholm argues that Gettier-style cases involve a proposition that is *defectively* evident for S, insofar as it is based on propositions which make evident a *false* proposition. According to Chisholm, any proposition that is known must be evident but not defectively evident. Chisholm provides a careful analysis of the concept 'defectively evident' and explains how this can be used to resolve Gettier counterexamples. Moreover, in "A Version of Foundationalism" (1980) Chisholm analyzes the *structure* of epistemic justification. Foundationalism, which Chisholm defends, is contrasted with coherentism, an alternative theory of the structure of justification. Together with efforts to meet the Gettier problem and analyze the (JTB) model of knowledge, friction over the correct model of the structure of epistemic justification, over foundationalism versus coherentism, has led to the recent development of virtue epistemology.

FOUNDATIONALISM/COHERENTISM

Foundationalism is the doctrine that knowledge is a system in which most beliefs are justified by other beliefs which serve as supporting evidence, while some beliefs are basic. A basic belief is a justified belief, which may serve as evidence for other beliefs, but which is not itself based on any other beliefs. Instead, basic beliefs are thought to be justified by such things as immediate perception or self-evidence. Foundationalism presents an architectural model of knowledge according to which the foundations of knowledge are basic beliefs, and such that all non-basic beliefs are ultimately supported by them.

Foundationalism seems to solve the so-called "regress problem for justification." Suppose we are trying to determine whether some epistemic subject S is mediately justified in believing some proposition p. If so, there must be other propositions, q, r… that S believes which constitute adequate grounds (or sufficient evidence) for p, and such that S is justified in believing them. But then, if S is not immediately justified in believing q, r …, there must be other propositions that S believes which constitute adequate grounds for q, r…; and so on. If this evidential chain terminates in an unjustified belief, then no belief supported by it is justified either. If the chain does not terminate, but goes on *ad infinitum*, conditions for justification do not obtain. On one hand, a finite agent is incapable of infinite beliefs, and on the other, there can be no *support relation* between S's belief that p and an infinite regression of beliefs. Only a regression of justified beliefs terminating in immediately justified belief provides justification for mediately justified beliefs. Thus, it seems, foundationalism is the only plausible model of the structure of epistemic justification.

The main challenge to foundationalism aims precisely at the status of putatively basic beliefs. What beliefs could constitute epistemic foundations? Do we really have immediate knowledge of any self-evident or perceptual beliefs? The coherence theory of justification arises precisely from dissatisfaction with this aspect of foundationalism. Coherentists reject the notion of immediate knowledge. One of the best presentations of coherentism as a theory of the structure of epistemic justification is Laurence BonJour's, *The Structure of Empirical Knowledge* (1985).

BonJour develops coherentism as an alternative way out of the regress problem mentioned above. He argues that instead of a chain of justifiers ending in immediate knowledge, ending in unjustified belief, or going on *ad infinitum*, the chain may form a loop. For any proposition p, then, p is justified only if it coheres with other justified beliefs in the ring. On this model, beliefs are justified (or not) by reference to the whole system of beliefs in which they are embedded. The coherence of the system is what confers justification on beliefs within the system. Of course, this amounts to saying that, ultimately, p is justified only if p is justified.

BonJour and other coherentists, however, accept circularity as a feature of the justification of beliefs. They argue, however, that there is an important distinction between vicious and non-vicious circularity, and that coherentism involves only a form of non-vicious circularity. In brief, circularity is vicious (logically untenable) if the structure of justification is linear and unidirectional. In that case, justification of the belief that p is conferred by other beliefs that stand in support relations to p. To suggest that the belief that p is involved in the justification of the belief that p *in this way* is to say that the belief that p supports itself. But it is precisely the idea that the structure of justification is linear and unidirectional that coherentism denies. Instead, coherentists make reference to a concept of "global justification." On this view, justification is holistic, involving a total system of beliefs. Coherence in an overall system of beliefs is what constitutes epistemic justification, according to coherentism.

As we shall see below, the intriguing debate over foundationalism and coherentism plays a major role in the development of virtue epistemology. Still, dispute over the correct model of the structure of evidential justification continues. For instance, BonJour was one of the most vigorous advocates of coherentism during the 1980s and 90s. However, in "Toward a Defense of Empirical Foundationalism" (2001) he writes:

> Foundationalism… has recently been subjected to incessant attack and has come to be widely regarded as an obviously untenable and even hopeless view… I myself have played a role in these developments, offering some of the arguments against foundationalism and attempting to develop and defend the coherentist alternative in particular. But having labored long in the intriguing but ultimately barren labyrinths of coherentism, I have come to the conviction that the recent antifoundationalist trend is a serious mistake, one that is taking epistemology… in largely the wrong direction and giving undeserved credibility to those who would reject epistemology altogether.[1]

---

[1] In *Resurrecting Old-Fashioned Foundationalism*, Michael R. DePaul (Ed.) (Lanham, MD: Rowman and Littlefield, 2001), 21-22.

Epistemic Normativity

In "Epistemology Naturalized" (1969), W. V. O. Quine advances the radical proposal that because we cannot justify empirical beliefs in any foundational way, we should abandon epistemology for cognitive psychology instead. We should, for example, study the nature of perception and belief processing instead of the justificatory status of perceptual beliefs. In this way, epistemology would become naturalized; it would be divested of normativity and made into a purely descriptive scientific enterprise.

While epistemologists are not uninterested in neuroscience and cognitive psychology, they generally resist the idea that epistemology should be reduced to psychology, and the epistemic properties of agents to psychological processes and empirically observable states. There are at least two reasons for this. First, there is a distinction between substantive epistemology which is concerned with the conditions under which S knows or is justified in believing that p, and meta-epistemology which investigates the concepts and methods involved in substantive epistemology—for example, the concept and structure of 'justification', and the concept 'knowledge' itself. Quine's claims about the failure of epistemology simply ignore the distinction, and with it the project of meta-epistemology which has been at the heart of analytic epistemology in the twentieth century. Second, as Hilary Putnam argues in "Why Reason Can't Be Naturalized" (1983), epistemology cannot be turned over to the sciences precisely because it is essentially a normative enterprise. Naturalizing epistemology would require eliminating the normative notions of *justification, warrant, epistemic desiderata, and good reasons*. Such a proposal is incoherent, Putnam argues, so long as we (rightly) construe truth as a correspondence relation of mind and world. That is to say, so long as we take beliefs (or propositions) to be true if and only if their propositional content corresponds to the way things are. The correspondence theory of truth presupposes the very normative notions that naturalism seeks to eliminate.

Virtue epistemology arises from reflection on the normative quality of knowledge. As we have seen, naturalism, internalism, and the analysis of the concept 'justification' have all raised issues concerning epistemic normativity—that is, the value-laden nature of epistemology. 'Justification' itself is a non-descriptive, non-factual evaluative concept. It expresses what in addition to true belief is *good* in the way of belief, or *good* from the epistemic point of view. It concerns what *ought* to hold between truth and belief. Insofar as justification—and a variety of epistemic desiderata—is necessary for knowledge, and knowledge is generally good for living well, 'epistemic justification' is a linchpin that connects ethics and epistemology in the broadest sense, namely, as aspects of philosophical reflection on value.

Epistemology of belief, which preoccupied so much of twentieth century epistemology, focuses on the normative properties of beliefs; for example, is the belief that p justified? This view presupposes that the normative properties of epistemic agents, or those who hold a belief, are derived from the normative properties of their beliefs. If the belief that p is justified, and S believes that p, then S is justified in believing that p. Virtue epistemology reverses this order of dependence. S's belief that p is justified (warranted, based on adequate grounds, or in other ways *good* from the epistemic point of view), if S, from the epistemic point of view, *ought* to believe that p. This matches a similar adjustment in contemporary virtue ethics. Modern moral philosophy emphasizes the normative quality of actions (do they maximize desirable consequences, are they obligatory, etc.). From this perspective, agent evaluation is dependent upon act evaluation. To simplify, a person who performs good acts is thereby a good person. By contrast, virtue ethics emphasizes the normative quality of agents (their character, motives, etc.). From this perspective, act evaluation is dependent upon agent evaluation. People of good character tend to do the right thing. Before we explore the similarities between virtue ethics and virtue epistemology, however, it will be useful to look more closely at how virtue epistemology grew out of the epistemology of belief.

Contemporary virtue epistemology begins with the publication of Ernest Sosa's "The Raft and the Pyramid: Coherence versus Foundations in the Theory of Knowledge" (1980). Sosa argues that the notion of intellectual virtues can resolve the impasse between foundationalism and coherentism as accounts of the structure of epistemic justification. Employing the metaphor of a pyramid, foundationalism sees the structure of justification in terms of nonsymmetrical support relations between levels; for example, the higher-level belief that driving tonight will be dangerous and the lower level belief about the weather forecast and its reliability. The lowest level has the special epistemic status of being a foundation, which supports all higher level nodes (propositions, beliefs) in the pyramid. These foundational beliefs or propositions, which are instances of immediate knowledge, are, paradigmatically, sensory experiences expressed in observation statements. Coherentism, on the other hand, employs the metaphor of a raft and depicts justification and knowledge as an un-tethered, fluid structure whose internal parts (propositions, beliefs) are bound together by logical or conceptual relations.

Sosa finds intractable problems with both models of the structure of justification. Briefly, the problem with coherentism is that it leaves a system of beliefs adrift, because perceptual beliefs are not, as it were, answerable to the world. That is to say, the justification of perceptual beliefs is, according to coherentism, entirely a function of logical relations. The problem is that we can take any perceptual belief in a coherent system—say, that my keyboard is before me on the desk—and assert its contradictory, and then make whatever small changes are necessary to preserve logical coherence with other propositions in the system. The result would be an alternative system of beliefs that "counts as knowledge" every bit as much as the original system did— while my sensory experience remains unchanged—it appears that my keyboard is before me on the desk. Surely, Sosa argues, a theory of knowledge that implies that I am justified in believing the proposition "My keyboard is on the desk" and that I am justified in believing its negation is untenable.

Foundationalism, by contrast, holds that a belief can be justified not only by its logical coherence within a system, but also, in cases of foundational beliefs, by its observational content *vis-à-vis* the use of the senses under standard conditions. The problem with foundationalism, according to Sosa, is that it rests on a dilemma. Sosa explains, "A simple question presents the foundationalist's dilemma: regarding the epistemic principle that underlies our justification for believing that something here is red on the basis of our visual experience of something red, is it proposed as a fundamental principle or as a derived generalization?"[5] If it is understood as a fundamental principle of justification, then "we would open the door to a multitude of equally basic principles with no unifying factor. There would be some for vision, some for hearing, etc., without even mentioning the corresponding extraterrestrial principles."[6] If, on the other hand, we think of the foundationalist's principles as a derived generalization, "then it would be quite unphilosophical to stop there" since an account of some deeper, unifying ground would still be wanting. Thus, the dilemma is that on either alternative, foundationalism cannot provide a unified account of what it is that confers justificatory status on basic (foundational) beliefs.

(It is worth noting that some foundationalists, including William Alston (1983) and Alvin Plantinga (1993a; 1993b) argue against Sosa that basic beliefs require no account of their justificatory status since they are instances of immediate knowledge. Alston (1991; 1996) and Plantinga (2000) argue that

---

[5] In *Human Knowledge*, Paul Moser and Arnold vander Nat (Eds.), (Oxford: Oxford University Press, 1987), 321.
[6] *Human Knowledge*, 322.

belief in God is or can be properly epistemically basic, and hence in no need of justification—a view that has come to be known as *reformed epistemology*.)

Sosa argues that virtue epistemology can overcome the impasse between foundationalism and coherentism by providing a unified account of justificatory status regarding both basic and non-basic beliefs; namely, an account of intellectual virtue or cognitive excellence. According to Sosa, intellectual virtues are "stable dispositions for belief acquisition, through their...contribution toward getting us to the truth."[7] That is to say, intellectual virtues are typically innate abilities (though they may also include some acquired habits) that enable cognitive agents to reliably gain the truth in matters that are relevant and important for them. On this account, justified belief is belief grounded in intellectual virtues, while knowledge is true belief so grounded.

We can see how this provides the general unified account of justification found wanting in foundationalism. For, a paradigm of intellectual virtue for human beings is, on Sosa's account, our visual system; a virtue relevant to the justificatory status of beliefs based on sensory experience. A reliable visual system constitutes a stable disposition for forming beliefs about the environment on the basis of sensory inputs. Logical coherence is another intellectual virtue conferring justification by augmenting reliability. In this way, a unified account of intellectual virtue preserves the truth in both foundationalism and coherentism while avoiding the pitfalls of each. This explanation of why beliefs grounded in intellectual virtues are justified is a unified account because it explains why all beliefs so grounded are likely to be true. Moreover, the distinction between intellectual virtues for forming beliefs about the environment on the basis of experiential inputs on one hand, and intellectual virtues for forming coherent systems of beliefs on the other, maps onto a distinction between what Sosa calls "animal knowledge" and "reflective knowledge" respectively.

Following Sosa, other advocates of virtue epistemology have argued that it can solve the Gettier problem, resolve the debate over internalism and externalism in epistemology, explain perceptual knowledge, and account for "high-grade" epistemic properties and concepts such as understanding and wisdom. Although he is motivated far more by interest in epistemology than virtue, Sosa is credited with returning virtue to epistemology.

---

[7] *Human Knowledge*, 323.

THE RISE OF VIRTUE EPISTEMOLOGY

Virtue epistemology is distinguished from belief-based epistemology. The latter takes beliefs to be the primary objects of epistemic evaluation, and justification and knowledge to be the primary evaluative properties and concepts. Within belief-based epistemology we may distinguish between propositional and doxastic justification. S is *propositionally* justified in believing that p if and only if S is in such a position that, if S were to believe that p, that belief would be justified. S is *doxastically* justified in believing that p if and only if S believes that p, and that belief is justified. In contrast, virtue epistemology takes the intellectual virtues and vices of cognitive *agents*—not beliefs—to be the fundamental properties and concepts in epistemology.

Lorraine Code is one early proponent of virtue epistemology who emphasizes the importance of epistemic agent-evaluation.[8] Code argues that focus on the virtue of epistemic responsibility fundamentally shifts the emphasis in epistemology in at least two ways. First, it shows that the contextual and social dimensions of knowledge must be taken into account. Second, it suggests that conceptual analysis is not the best way to advance our understanding of intellectual virtue. Instead, in line with Alasdair MacIntyre's approach to ethical virtue, Code suggests that narrative is necessary to help advance understanding of intellectual virtue and vice.

Christopher Hookway (2003) argues that the goal of analytic epistemology is too narrow, and that a systematic or theoretical account of justification or knowledge is beside the point.[9] In this way, Hookway views epistemology in a way analogous to the so-called anti-theorists in virtue ethics discussed above.[10] Hookway and Code characterize one trend in virtue epistemology away from rigorist analyses of thin concepts such as 'justification'. Instead they urge a more open and diffuse approach to knowledge involving thick concepts of intellectual virtue and vice. Such anti-theory is outside of the mainstream of current virtue epistemology, however. Instead, virtue epistemologists generally sustain analytical interest in 'justification' and 'knowledge' as well as the nature of the intellectual virtues.

---

[8] *Epistemic Responsibility* (Hanover, NH: University Press of New England, 1987).

[9] How to be a Virtue Epistemologist in *Intellectual Virtue*. DePaul and Zagzebski (Eds.), (Oxford: Oxford University Press, 2003).

[10] See Stanley E. Clarke and Evan Simpson, Anti-*Theory in Ethics and Moral Conservatism* (New York: State University of New York Press, 1989).

74 Daniel P. Haggerty

Two theories have recently emerged, namely, "virtue-reliabilism" and "virtue-responsibilism".

VIRTUE-RELIABILISM

Leading virtue-reliabilists include Ernest Sosa (1991), Alvin Goldman (1992), and John Greco (2000). A sketch of Sosa's version may be taken as generally representative of virtue-reliabilism.

Sosa's account of intellectual virtue grew out of process-reliabilism, which itself grew out of externalist responses to the Gettier problem and other problems with internalism in the epistemology of belief. Process-reliabilists argue that a belief's being based on a reliable belief forming process is sufficient for its justification. A reliable process is one that would tend to produce a preponderance of true beliefs over false beliefs in the long run. The justificatory status of such processes obtains irrespective of whether agents have introspective access to the processes and their epistemic status.

In *Knowledge in Perspective* (1991), Sosa develops his account of intellectual virtues in order to solve certain problems facing process-reliabilism; namely, problems of range and context. Sosa argues that the virtues are reliable faculties vis-à-vis particular fields of propositions, and under particular conditions. Thus 20/20 vision, for instance, is reliable regarding a limited range of propositions under certain conditions—say, propositions whose content ranges over a restricted domain of colors and shapes under certain conditions regarding distance, light, etc. In this way, the intellectual virtue of 20/20 vision is defined in terms of a disposition to produce a preponderance of true beliefs about the basic colors and shapes of medium-sized objects that are nearby and in good light without obstruction.[11] In this way, Sosa conceives of virtue as *excellent function*.

Intellectual virtues thus conceived are natural or innate. Their epistemic value is strictly instrumental. They are valuable because they are a reliable means for attaining truth, which is valuable in itself. Though he concedes that some secondary intellectual virtues may be derived, he contends that the "truly fundamental virtues may be largely innate."[12] Fundamental intellectual virtues include well-functioning vision, hearing, memory, induction, deduction, and introspection, according to Sosa. Furthermore, he argues that the concept of

---

[11] Ernest Sosa, *Knowledge in Perspective* (New York: Cambridge University Press, 1991), 139. .
[12] *Knowledge in Perspective*, 278.

virtue applies to anything admitting of a functional analysis. As he explains, "The eye does, after all, have its virtues, and so does the knife."[13] It is the qualities of an entity that enable it to perform its given functions well that, on Sosa's virtue-reliabilist view, constitute its virtues. And thus it is the qualities of epistemic agents enabling them to perform their function as epistemic agents well that constitute their intellectual virtues, where "functioning well" means attaining a preponderance of true beliefs.

In this way, Sosa provides an analysis of justification and a theory of knowledge: justified belief is belief that is appropriately grounded in intellectual virtues; and knowledge is true belief that is so grounded. He takes this as giving the unified account of justification and knowledge that had been sought after in belief-based epistemology, while meeting objections from Gettier problems as well as "other cognitive beings" problems. Justification and knowledge for other cognitive beings would depend upon their innate or natural intellectual virtues (e.g., echolocation in bats), and the sensory inputs they process.

VIRTUE-RESPONSIBILISM

In characteristically externalist fashion, virtue-reliabilists conceive of the intellectual virtues as natural faculties that promote cognitive excellence. Paradigms of such faculties include sense perception, memory, and inferential processing. By contrast, virtue-responsibilists typically model their analyses of intellectual virtues on Aristotle's analysis of moral virtue, conceiving of them as *acquired* traits of character; namely, the dispositions a responsible inquirer would have. Accordingly, virtue-responsibilists argue that acquiring intellectual virtues requires deliberative choice. Paradigms of intellectual virtue from this perspective include intellectual honesty, courage, and openness.

Linda Zagzebski (1996) and James Montmarquet (1993) are among the principal proponents of virtue-reliabilism. Both think that intellectual virtues are acquired traits of character, and that possessing intellectual virtues requires having appropriate epistemic motivations—a desire to gain the truth and avoid falsity. They differ over how they connect choosing the mean with reliability. For Montmarquet, though he concedes that the virtues may produce a preponderance of true beliefs, he explicitly denies that the intellectual virtues

---

[13] *Knowledge in Perspective*, 271.

require reliability, arguing instead that in a Cartesian demon-world, traits like open-mindedness could still hit the mean and be virtuous, even though they would be unreliable. Zagzebski disagrees, arguing instead that intellectual virtues are acquired traits that require both appropriate epistemic motivation and reliable success in producing a preponderance of true beliefs.[14] We may take a sketch of Zagzebski's views as generally representative of virtue-responsibilism.

Like Montmarquet, Zagzebski models her analysis of intellectual virtue on Aristotle's account of moral virtue. Unlike virtue-reliabilists, Zagzebski contends that the virtues are not natural or innate, but acquired and enduring traits of character. She writes, "A virtue is a deep quality of a person, closely identified with her selfhood, whereas natural faculties are only the raw materials for the self."[15] Accordingly, as acquired qualities that are closely identified with selfhood, virtues (whether intellectual or moral) are traits or properties that deserve *praise* (for being acquired) and *blame* (for not being acquired) in a way natural faculties do not. Of course we sometimes praise natural faculties, such as excellent vision, and the results they produce. In so doing, however, we are not praising the agent for acquiring them, nor even for possessing them, since nobody can be credited for possessing what is innate. Moreover, we do not ordinarily blame agents or their faculties for defects. We do not fault the myopic people for their near-sightedness, nor do we fault their eyes. Yet, we do praise agents for possessing a virtue precisely because we credit them (at least in part) with the acquisition of it.

Further, Zagzebski distinguishes intellectual virtues from skills. Like virtues, skills are acquired. One difference, however, is that skills are capacities that may or may not be exercised on any given occasion. A skillful tennis player, for example, may hold back when playing someone who is new to the game. By contrast, a person cannot be said to have acquired a virtue unless it is exercised on the appropriate occasions. A second difference between skills and virtues is that the former do not require any particular motivational structure for their acquisition. Intellectual virtues, by contrast, are, according to Zagzebski, acquired as a result of being motivated by love for truth. Here is a shortened list of Zagzebski's intellectual virtues and intellectual skills which exhibit the distinction:

Intellectual Virtues:
- ability to recognize salient facts; sensitivity to detail

---

[14] See Linda Zagzebski, *Virtues of the Mind: An Inquiry into the Nature of Virtue and the Ethical Foundations of Knowledge* (New York: Cambridge University Press, 1996), 137.
[15] *Virtues of the Mind*, 104.

- open-mindedness in collecting and appraising evidence
- fairness in evaluating the arguments of others
- intellectual humility
- intellectual perseverance, diligence, care, and thoroughness

Intellectual Skills:

- verbal skills: skills of speaking and writing
- perceptual acuity skills
- logical skills
- mathematical skills and skills of quantitative reasoning
- mechanical skills[16]

According to Zagzebski, intellectual virtues have a two-fold motivational component: (1) an underlying motivation for "cognitive contact with reality," which generates (2) a motivation specific to the particular virtue in question. The motivation for cognitive contact with reality connects with the motivation for truth; that is, the love of truth for its own sake. Their love of truth, according to Zagzebski, generates motivations that are distinctive to the various intellectual virtues. So, love of truth motivates the virtue of epistemic fairness in evaluating the arguments of others, the virtue of epistemic humility in assessing the status of one's own beliefs, and so on.

While possessing the appropriate motivational component is necessary for intellectual virtue, it is not, according to Zagzebski, sufficient. It is at this point that Zagzebski diverges from Montmarquet and other virtue-responsibilists. In addition to having the appropriate motivation, Zagzebski contends that one must also be reliably successful in attaining the ends towards which her motives are directed. Otherwise, one cannot be said to possess intellectual virtue. This is because, following Aristotle on the notion of *ethical* virtue, Zagzebski insists that virtue is a success notion; it involves both a motivational component and a reliable success component. So, for example, one must be motivated to be fair in evaluating the arguments of others because one loves the truth, and one must be reliably successful in being fair in one's evaluations and at attaining true beliefs as a result.

So, present accounts of the intellectual virtues claim that they involve reliability, motivation for truth, or both. Sosa and other virtue-reliabilists claim that reliability is sufficient for justification. On this view, motives and other

---

[16] *Virtues of the Mind*, 114.

inner states are not constitutive of intellectual virtue. Montmarquet argues that virtuous motivation is sufficient for justification. Reliable success is not necessary. Zagzebski claims that motivation for the truth and reliable success are necessary and jointly sufficient, so that knowledge is a state of true belief (cognitive contact with reality) arising out of acts of intellectual virtue.

All of the views sketched above involve far more complexity than is presented here. Some virtue-epistemologists, such as Greco (2000), are not easily characterized as strictly virtue-reliabilists rather than virtue-responsibilists, since, like Zagzebski, Greco ties intellectual virtue to responsibility without rejecting reliabilism. Still, this rough sketch provides a road map to several key locations on an emerging conceptual terrain in contemporary analytic epistemology. It also serves to set up the connections between ethics and epistemology discussed in the next chapter.

Chapter 5

EPISTEMOLOGY AND ETHICS

We have seen why epistemology and ethics came apart in modern philosophy, and why they were kept apart in early analytic philosophy. We have also seen how they have been brought back in touch with the rise of virtue ethics, and then virtue epistemology in recent analytic philosophy. Up to this point, then, we have been concerned primarily with intellectual geography—a study of the features and atmosphere of ethics and epistemology over three hundred years, and how these have been affected by philosophical and other intellectual activity. This chapter presents an argument. Based on insights from Aristotle and John McDowell, I aim to show that ethics and epistemology are truly inseparable.

Early analytic philosophers saw the Enlightenment as effectively driving a wedge between ethics and epistemology. Hume's insights and arguments developed within the emerging modern scientific worldview of 18th century Europe. The perceived power of scientific explanation was wrangling with the social and political power and influence of Christianity and the Church. In that context, Hume and the modern scientific method dichotomized science and ethics. Against a longstanding doctrine that the universe was morally ordered and that this order was discernible by reason—a moral order presumed to be every bit as factual as any observation statement in the natural sciences—Hume argued that moral life is fundamentally constituted by human feeling and passion.

The ultimate aim of Hume's project consists of valuing human liberation and empowerment. Such a goal was not new to philosophy. Plato, for example, also roots his philosophy in freedom. Unlike Hume, however, Plato conceives of reason and objectivity, not feeling and passion, as the source of human liberation. Against being swept along unreflectively with too little reason, against being manipulated by sophist, poet, and politician and their appeals to sentiment, Plato argues that the individual and society are liberated and empowered by exercising reason in the pursuit of truth. While Plato prescribes balance and harmony among the passions and appetites ruled by reason, as with Hume, Plato's legacy is sometimes distorted. There is a tendency to take from Plato the idea that if a little more reason and a little less passion and appetite are good, a lot more reason and a lot less passion are even better. The result is a distorted picture of Plato as a champion of reason over against all emotion and desire.

For Hume, freedom is found in passion and subjectivity. Against being pushed along unreflectively with too little feeling, against being manipulated by the theologian, the philosopher, and the man of science with their appeals to Reason—to the universal, the factual, and the objective—the individual and society are liberated and empowered by their individual subjectivity and passion. By dichotomizing natural facts (Reason) and moral sentiment (passion), Hume calls for a more open, tolerant, liberal, democratic society. This is quite contrary, however, to how Hume is sometimes interpreted, not least of all in early analytic philosophy. In that reading of Hume, because the value and knowledge-producing power of modern science are indisputable, and because ethics is not science, ethics is not knowledge-producing—nor, perhaps, is it valuable.

What Plato and Hume have in common is a commitment to human liberation. Moreover, they both locate the opportunity for human advancement at the intersection of ethics and epistemology, albeit in different ways. Plato's antidote to the tyranny of the multitude was a transcendentalism of objective, immutable truths—an anti-skeptical, anti-relativistic absolute reality. Hume's antidote to the tyranny of religion, government, philosophy and science, was a tincture of pyrrhonist skepticism and a strong dose of subjectivity and passion.

Where are the intersections of ethics and epistemology in present analytic or post-analytic philosophy? This is a vital question that is just lately beginning to take form.[1] Here I argue for two important points of contact. First, ethics and epistemology share a common source of normativity, namely, *reasons that are answerable to the world.* Second, ethics and epistemology share ultimate aims.

---

[1] For a good start see *Intellectual Virtue: Perspectives from Ethics and Epistemology*, Michael DePaul and Linda Zagzebski, (Eds.) (New York: Oxford University Press, 2003).

A COMMON SOURCE OF NORMATIVITY

In the wake of Hume, early analytic philosophy sent ethics off with religion and metaphysics to the domain of sentimental and speculative nonsense, while epistemology was elevated to an investigation of knowledge in the sciences. Across Hume's fact/value divide, epistemology was conceived of as philosophy pertaining to matters of fact—of whether and how observation statements are knowable. Emotivism in analytic ethics conceived of moral statements as lacking any cognitive content, while logical empiricism sought to ground knowledge in the meaningfulness of observation statements. This trend was continued in analytic epistemology of belief, particularly in versions of foundationalism where the paradigm of knowledge is perceptual belief.

At the same time, a strong undercurrent pulled epistemology back in the direction of the normative. Recall Quine's (1969) effort to naturalize epistemology and reduce it to cognitive psychology, which was met with strong resistance from within epistemology. The friction caused epistemologists to recognize and develop 'epistemic justification' as a *normative* concept. If epistemic justification is normative, and justification is necessary for knowledge, then knowledge is normative and cannot be reduced to descriptive science. Like 'justification', 'epistemic desiderata' and 'intellectual virtues' are non-descriptive, evaluative concepts. They express what is *good* in the way of belief, or *good* from the epistemic point of view. With such concepts we cannot give an account of the conditions for knowledge, including knowledge in the natural sciences, without an account of *valuing*.

At the heart of the modern separation of knowledge and value is a dichotomization of the natural and the normative. The tendency to dichotomize them is strong for reasons already adduced, including Hume's arguments, the power of modern natural-scientific explanation, and the desire to be free from socially and politically oppressive conceptions of a morally ordered universe. The dichotomy is false, however. The natural and the normative do not fall under two sharply distinct categories. Resisting the false dichotomy is essential to reconciling ethics and epistemology.

We see that the natural and the normative are inextricable when we attend to a most primary, remarkable fact about human existence, namely, that valuing is the most fundamental point of human cognitive contact with reality. It is the reason for the relation of mind to world. Unlike other species for which survival is the point of contact between consciousness and environment,

82   Daniel P. Haggerty

human animals also appraise the value of experience. We do not have access to a ready-made, value-free "objective world" copied in experience. Rather, valuing is precisely the context in the light of which mind and world are related.

The centrality of the normative in the relation of mind and world is brought out clearly and explicitly by John McDowell:

> To make sense of a mental state's or episode's being directed towards the world, in the way in which, say, a belief or judgment is, we need to put the state or episode in a normative context. A belief or judgment to the effect that things are thus and so—a belief or judgment whose content (as we say) is that things are thus and so—must be a posture or stance that is *correctly* or *incorrectly* adopted according to whether or not things are indeed thus and so. (If we can make sense of a judgment or belief as directed towards the world in that way, other kinds of content-bearing postures or stances should easily fall into place.) This relation between mind and world is normative, then, in this sense: thinking that aims at judgment, or the fixation of belief, is answerable to the world—to how things are—for whether or not it is correctly executed.[2]

McDowell restricts the claim that our thinking is answerable to the world to the idea that our thinking is answerable to the empirical world, not because he denies abstract thinking, but for the Kantian reason that we first confront the world by way of sensory perception. It is in this sense, then, that our thinking is answerable to experience. *Being answerable to* experience—that is to say, nature and the empirical world delivering a *verdict* on our beliefs and judgments—forces the idea that, against an absolute objective conception of THE WORLD, experience constitutes, as Quine puts it, a "tribunal" mediating the ways in which our thinking is responsible to how things are.

What does it mean to say that experience constitutes a tribunal—a space where our beliefs are answerable to the world, a place where verdicts of correct or incorrect belief are delivered? How does such a conception of the empirical tie together the natural and the normative?

In his celebrated attack on what he calls "the Myth of the Given" (in experience), Wilfred Sellars writes: "In characterizing an episode or a state as that of *knowing*, we are not giving an empirical description of that episode or state; we are placing it in the logical space of reasons, or justifying and being

---

[2] *Mind and World* (Cambridge: Harvard University Press, 1996), xi-xii.

Epistemology and Ethics

able to justify what one says."[3] Sellars distinguishes concepts that are only intelligible in the logical space of reasons, concepts whose intelligibility depends upon their being placed in a normative context, from concepts that can be employed in empirical description or observation statements. McDowell upholds the distinction, "understanding 'empirical description' as placing things in the logical space of nature..."[4]

What is the logical space of nature? McDowell:

> I think we capture the essentials of Sellars' thinking if we take it that the logical space of nature is the logical space in which the natural sciences function, as we have been enabled to conceive them by a well-charted, and in itself admirable, development of modern thought. We might say that to place something in nature on the relevant conception, as contrasted with placing it in the logical space of reasons, is to situate it in the realm of law. But what matters for Sellars's point is not that or any other positive characterization, but the negative claim: whatever the relations are that constitute the logical space of nature, they are *different in kind* from the normative relations that constitute the logical space of reasons. The relations that constitute the logical space of nature, on the relevant conception, do not include relations such as one thing's being warranted, or—for the general case—correct, in the light of another.[5]

The relations that constitute the logical space of reasons, on the other hand, do include one thing's being *justified* in the light of another. Such relations comprise epistemic desiderata, including the intellectual virtues. This is the logical space of epistemology, the space in which one thing serves as reason for another, one belief counts as evidence in support of another. As such, this is also precisely the logical space of normativity, the context in which answerability to the world and the tribunal of experience obtain.

McDowell's own position on the dichotomy of logical spaces is crucial here for understanding the connection between the normative and the natural, and between ethics and epistemology in the broadest and deepest sense. It is helpful to quote him at length.

> The modern scientific revolution made possible a newly clear conception of the distinctive kind of intelligibility that the natural sciences allow us to

---

[3] "Empiricism and the Philosophy of Mind," *Minnesota Studies in the Philosophy of Science* volume 1. Herbert Feigl and Michael Scriven (Eds.). Minneapolis: University of Minnesota Press, 1956), 298-299. Quoted in McDowell, *Mind and World*, xiv.

[4] *Mind and World*, xiv.

[5] *Mind and World*, xiv-xv.

find in things. The new clarity consists largely, I claim, in an appreciation of something close to what underlies Sellars's warning of a naturalistic fallacy (in epistemology). We must sharply distinguish natural-scientific intelligibility from the kind of intelligibility something acquires when we situate it in the logical space of reasons. That is a way of affirming the dichotomy of logical spaces... Even so, we can acknowledge that the idea of experience is the idea of something natural, without thereby removing the idea of experience from the logical space of reasons. What makes this possible is that we need not identify the dichotomy of logical spaces with a dichotomy between the *natural* and the normative. We need not equate the very idea of nature with the idea of instantiations of concepts that belong in the logical space—admittedly separate, on this view, from the logical space of reasons—in which the natural-scientific kind of intelligibility is brought to light.[6]

Natural-scientific intelligibility operates in the logical space of nature, where reasons and justification do not obtain. Instead, this is the realm of observation and description augmented by mathematical precision. Nevertheless, the idea of nature that animates this logical space is also operative in the logical space of reasons, a normative context in which reasons and justification are central.

My thesis is this: Epistemology—the theory of knowledge—itself belongs to the logical space of *reasons*, the *normative context* in which experience is relevant to knowledge insofar as it is used as reasons in support of belief. Moreover, as valuing is the primary context in which mind and world are related, the logical space of nature is derivative from the logical space of reasons. The very idea of the world to which our natural-scientific thoughts are *answerable* is an idea upon which the logical space of nature is itself based.

Recall Newton's universal law of gravitation. It is a purely descriptive account belonging to the logical space of nature. Newton offers no explanation of the *cause* of gravitation. Instead, he identifies the phenomena of gravity (observation) and describes those phenomena with mathematical precision. The universal law of gravitation is an excellent example of the kind of intelligibility that belongs to the logical space of nature. Formulations of the law involve the instantiations of concepts that belong in the logical space in which the distinctive kind of intelligibility that the natural sciences allow us to find in things is brought to light. Newton never assigns or hypothesizes a cause

---

[6] *Mind and World*, xix.

Epistemology and Ethics 85

of or reasons for gravitational force. He observes and describes it. As such, the universal law of gravity does not belong to the logical space of *reasons*.

Gravitational force is germane to epistemology—and in this way, relevant to knowledge—when it is situated in the logical space of *reasons*. When we *apply* the law to predict and interpret the behavior of bodies with spatial extent, as opposed to the theoretical bodies employed in the formulation of the law, we assert that the proportion and distribution of the mass of a body, for example, *causes* the force to behave in such and such ways. Here 'gravitation' acquires epistemic status. It is employed as a reason in support of belief.

In the logical space of reasons, the propositional content of statements about gravitational force serves as evidence in support of other propositions. Those propositions and the evidential support for them are then answerable to the world of experience. They are answerable to the tribunal of experience; as such, they are situated in a thoroughly *normative* context. It is a normative context, the logical space of reasons, in which the concepts 'nature', 'experience', and 'scientific explanation' are instantiated. Observation statements serve as basic beliefs in a foundational structure of justification just when they are imported from the logical space of nature into the space of reasons.

(In logic, the Boolean interpretation of universal propositions carries no existential import. The Aristotelian interpretation of universal statements does carry existential import. As such, the Boolean interpretation is suitable for organization in the logical space of nature, while the Aristotelian interpretation is suitable for drawing inferences and offering reasons in the logical space of reasons.)

Contrary to the early analytic split between ethics and metaphysics on the one hand, and epistemology and empirical science on the other, 'epistemic justification' and other evaluative epistemic concepts necessary for knowledge are instantiated in the normative context of reasons. This is the very same logical space in which the concepts 'intellectual virtue' and 'character virtue' get instantiated. Just as we appeal to 'nature' and 'experience' in a normative context of scientific or empirical explanation, so we can, and should, appeal to 'experience' and 'nature' in ethical reasoning and characterological explanations. *Reasons* are normative, whether they are scientific or ethical reasons, and as such they are *answerable* to the world. Hence, ethical reasons must be answerable to the world too.

ARISTOTLE ON ETHICAL AND INTELLECTUAL VIRTUES : THE ULTIMATE AIM

One point of contact between ethics and epistemology is the logical space of reasons they share. A second is the ultimate aims they have in common. This final section identifies some of those ultimate aims.[7]

Recall that *aretē* is translated from Greek through Latin into English as "virtue." In the proper philosophical sense of the term, virtue is an excellence which renders its possessor "an outstanding specimen of its kind."[8] Virtue-reliabilists take 'intellectual virtue' to refer to well-developed reliable faculties, such as 20/20 vision or an exceptional memory. By contrast, virtue-responsibilists take the concept 'intellectual virtue' to refer to a trait that can be acquired and developed by deliberate choice, thus constituting something the agent is more or less responsible for possessing. To put it plainly, responsibilists hold that intellectual virtues are to some extent up to us. Reliabilists think they are not. It is with the responsibilists' conception of intellectual virtue that I am concerned here. It is the concept closest to Aristotle's view of intellectual virtues.

In *Nicomachean Ethics* and *Posterior Analytics*, Aristotle identifies five intellectual virtues. These are the five ways the soul arrives at the truth by affirmation and denial. They include *sophia* (wisdom), *epistēmē* (pure science or knowledge for its own sake), *nous* (intelligence or intuitive understanding), *phronesis* (practical judgment), and *technē* (skill or craft knowledge). He distinguishes theoretical intelligence, those powers of the soul by which we know and understand, from practical intelligence, those powers of the soul by which we deliberate, plan, strategize, and chart a course of action (1143a35-b5). In addition to this distinction between practical and theoretical intellectual virtues, Aristotle distinguishes intellectual virtues generally from character virtues. The former are the stable conditions of the soul by which we attain the truth, the latter are stable conditions of the soul by which we attain *eudaimonia* (happiness).

These are conceptual distinctions, however. They help us to sort out and analyze different kinds of human excellences. To be sure, they can map on to real psychological differences. We can easily imagine someone who possesses excellent technical skill but lacks excellent character. Indeed, character vice and technical excellence is a lethal combination. There is no reason, however,

---

[7] I thank Joanna Klimaski for helpful discussion here.
[8] Sachs, *NE*, 212.

Epistemology and Ethics

to suppose that intellectual and ethical virtues are necessarily distinct, or discrete. To the contrary, Aristotle argues that in practice intellectual and ethical virtues mutually commission each other.

Ethical virtues are active conditions of the soul concerned with feelings and actions. They have correlative vices of excess and deficiency. These active conditions are a result of a deliberative desire, a choice, which the ethically virtuous person makes correctly. The source of virtuous action, then, is choice, which itself is a desire combined with a rational understanding that aims at some goal. In order to carry out these choices correctly, one must achieve correct thinking. As Aristotle puts it, "there is no choice without intellect and thinking, or without an active condition of character, since in action there is no such thing as doing well or the opposite without thinking and character" (1139a35-36). This "correct thinking" is practical judgment (*phronesis*), an intellectual virtue that governs action by making determinations about what is good or bad for a person (1140b5-6). As Aristotle explains:

> Practical judgment is linked together with virtue of character, and it with practical judgment, if the sources of practical judgment are dependent upon virtues of character, while the right thing belonging to virtues of character is dependent upon practical judgment (1178a15).[9]

Virtuous character manifests in choosing virtuous action. Such choice requires "correct thinking". In order to develop correct thinking as a stable condition, one must have a foundation of good character. Without good character, right action is vacuous, for one may be merely astute at doing the right things for the wrong reasons (1144a21-27).

If the above seems circular, we must recall that Aristotle's notion of what is *up to us* is not conceived of in terms of isolated individualism. The foundation of good character that is necessary for correct thinking need not be a foundation located exclusively in one's own character. Rather than circular, Aristotle's account is developmental and social. The development of correct thinking and good character mutually condition one another, and both are taught and reinforced (or not) by other people.

Aristotle's explanation of how virtues are acquired further supports the connection between ethical and intellectual virtues. According to Aristotle,

---

[9] Sachs, *NE*, 193. Here is the Ross translation: "Practical wisdom....is linked to excellence of character, and this to practical wisdom, since the principles of practical wisdom are in accordance with the moral excellences and rightness in the moral excellences is in accordance with practical wisdom."

"excellence of thinking is for the most part, both in its coming to be and in its growth, a result of teaching, for which reason it has need of experience and time, while excellence of character comes into being as a consequence of habit" (1103a11-14).[10] Of course, teaching and habituation are not disconnected. Children develop ethical virtue *via* habituation. Habit, though, is not exclusively responsible for character development; character is also instigated by a rational source, namely, parents, teachers, and other mentors. Children pick up upon and internalize ethical virtue because of intellectual virtue at work in these knowledgeable sources. Good parents and teachers praise the child when he exhibits virtuous behavior, leading the child to associate virtuous activity with pleasure. As the child begins to establish basic good character, he is then in a position to develop intellectual virtue, whereby he begins to understand the purpose of acting virtuously and to choose it deliberately and for its own sake. Such activity is then accompanied and perfected by pleasure that is not dependent upon external sources of praise.

Further, in his discussion of *epistēmē* Sachs explains that knowledge is a necessary component of deliberative choice. This can be seen by a reconsideration of character virtues. Virtues of character pertain to feelings and actions. The source of action is choice, which itself is a desire plus a rational understanding that aims at some goal—that is, a motivation. In other words, a choice is a deliberative desire (1111b5-1113a14). Because thought by itself moves nothing (1139a39), it is the combination of thought and deliberative desire (choice) that generates human action. Consequently, the source of virtuous action is intellect fused with feeling and desire (1139b5), which means that good thinking is a necessary component of virtuous character. In this way, knowledge is indeed constitutive of choosing good actions. So, if knowledge is a necessary component of deliberative choice, and if intellect is a basis for virtuous action, then epistemic capacities figure directly in ethical matters.

The above explains a deep psychological and conceptual connection between human knowledge and ethics. Hume, modern science, and early analytic philosophy notwithstanding, the two are inseparable. What binds them together psychologically and conceptually is, as Aristotle shows, virtue.

Intellectual and ethical virtues are connected as principles of the human soul. Aristotle distinguishes ethical and intellectual virtues as a result of their correspondence to different powers of the rational soul. Most generally, Aristotle distinguishes non-rational powers of the soul (nutritive, locomotive,

---

[10] Sachs, *NE*, 21.

Epistemology and Ethics

and perceptive) from rational powers (theoretical and practical reasoning). The rational he further divides into that which obeys reason and that which itself thinks (1139a4-15). The virtue or excellence of each division consists of the best active condition of each, that is, the condition in which each power functions excellently (1139a15-17). Ethical virtues pertain to feelings and action, which involve the principle of the soul that is rational in that it can be attentive to reason, even though it is not capable of deliberating. Intellectual virtues, on the other hand, are excellences of thinking and deliberation, that which itself reasons and produces beliefs. These conceptual distinctions notwithstanding, however, the close association and cooperation between the two rational principles of the soul and the two corresponding kinds of virtue renders them practically inseparable.

Finally, intellectual and ethical virtues are connected in relation to our ultimate aims. It is precisely in the context of elucidating the ultimate aim for human beings that Aristotle analyzes intellectual and ethical virtues in the first place. The elucidation takes place over the course of the *Nicomachean Ethics* as a whole. Aristotle begins the inquiry with an effort to advance understanding of what our ultimate aim should be. An ultimate aim must be such that it is chosen for its own sake, never as a means to another goal, and it must be self-sufficient, or choice worthy and lacking in nothing (1097a25-1097b22). He argues that the human good does not consist of mere contentment and intermittent pleasures (although pleasure does complete and perfect our ultimate end). Instead, the human good is a kind of activity.

(These preliminary considerations of 'ultimate aims' are necessary to eliminate lifestyles that "the many" commonly assume to be the good. According to Aristotle, the good and the ultimate aim for a human being is not a life devoted to pleasure alone, since this would be a slavish life dominated by desires. It is not a life of honor, since honor is pursued for the sake of being virtuous and nothing that pursues a greater goal can be the best. Nor is it a life of wealth because wealth is only a means to something greater and therefore is not sufficient.[11])

Aristotle concludes that the highest human good must be *eudaimonia*, for happiness is the end toward which secondary goods (pleasure, honor and wealth) aim. *Eudaimonia*, he reasons, is not a matter of obtaining external goods. It is rather something connected to the human function or primary human work (*ergon*), and therefore must be measured in the light of the nature and composition of a human being and his life. We will be in an active

---

[11] Sir David Ross, *Aristotle* (London: Methuen and Co. Ltd., 1923), 190.

90   Daniel P. Haggerty

condition of being-well, working or functioning maximally, as a result of actively fulfilling our potential as human beings.

Ergon is often translated as "function," but the more accurate and authentic rendition is "work." This translation, Martin Ostwald explains, allows a dual sense of the word, namely, a functional sense (a hammer's "work" is to drive in nails), as well as a concrete sense (the "works" of poets and artisans).[12] Joe Sachs adds that the conventional translation "function" is an inadequate rendering because it conceals the active sense of the word, the sense of what a human life is ultimately for; that is, a human being's life beyond merely "staying alive and leaving offspring."[13] In this sense, then, our ultimate aim is our "life's "work."

As we have seen, phronesis is indispensible for *eudaimonia*. But practical judgment is not the only intellectual virtue. Thinking does not exist exclusively for the work of practical judgment. Science, intuitive understanding, and wisdom are also intellectual virtues. Aristotle contends that theoretical wisdom, which combines science and intuitive understanding, is constitutive of happiness by being a part of virtue (1144a3-6), and that practical judgment may help secure the development of theoretical wisdom by issuing commands for its sake (1145a8-11). In this way, all of the intellectual virtues are bound up with the ultimate aim of being human, the human good—*eudaimonia*. In this way, happiness is the ultimate aim of both intellectual and ethical virtues.

Eudaimonia is not, however, Aristotle's only account of an ultimate aim. Nor does theoretical wisdom exist exclusively in relation to practical judgment. Instead, Aristotle contends that, "It is strange if someone thinks that politics or practical wisdom [ethics] is the most excellent kind of knowledge, unless man is the best thing in the cosmos" (1141a20-22). This striking remark implies that if human beings are the best thing in the cosmos, then *eudaimonia* the highest ultimate aim; but if there is something better than man then there is an even better ultimate aim. The name of such an ultimate aim is *makarios*.

In *Nicomachean Ethics*, Aristotle inquires into the ultimate aim of *human* life, as opposed to any other life, whether plants or gods. *Makarios* names not human happiness, but divine happiness. In "Divine and Human Happiness in Nicomachean Ethics," Stephen Bush presents what he calls a dualistic reading of Aristotle's two types of happiness.[14] The difference between them

---

[12] *Nicomachean Ethics*, Martin Ostwald (Trans.) (Indianapolis: The Bobbs-Merrill Company, Inc., 1962), 307.
[13] Sachs, *NE*, vii.
[14] *Philosophical Review* (2008) 117 (1), 49-75.

Epistemology and Ethics 91

corresponds to Aristotle's distinction between the characteristic human good and the highest good attainable.[15] The characteristic human good is human happiness (*eudaimonia*); the highest good attainable is divine happiness (*makarios*), also translated as blessedness. The characteristically human good is determined by human being-at-work, that which sets human beings apart from other species. Our characteristic being-at-work involves the full activity of our affective and rational capacities, our feelings and actions and our thinking.

Divine happiness is a greater good and ultimate aim. Though it is not the characteristically human good, according to Aristotle, human beings can achieve this good, owing to our possession of divine capacities, such as *nous* (intelligence or intuitive understanding). *Theōria* (contemplation) is the being-at-work of the intellect (*nous*), a thinking that is like seeing, complete at every instant. Such contemplation is not step-by-step thinking. It does not produce knowledge in the sense of arriving at something new. It is, as I say, not epistemic. It does not belong to the logical space of reasons, as explained above. It is, rather, an activity of the intellect that requires calming down out of distraction and settling into the contemplative relation to things (247b17-18).[16] Such activity is nevertheless a characteristically *divine* good. To whatever extent human beings do use intellect towards an ultimate aim, the characteristically human and more common aim is *eudaimonia*—happiness, practical wisdom, ethics and politics. These two ultimate aims, however, human and divine, are not, according to Aristotle, opposed:

> In introducing happiness as (*makarios*)....in 10.7, Aristotle is not offering an account of happiness to compete with that introduced in 1.7; rather, he is employing some of the same criteria used to identify the highest human good in 1.7, to identify the divine good, and also informing us that the divine good is attainable by humans.[17]

Knowledge by way of explanation, as distinguished from pure observation and description, and knowledge for the sake of anything beyond itself, belongs to the logical space of reasons. This is the logical space in which concepts that belong to scientific and ethical explanations get instantiated. It is the logical space of ethics and epistemology. The normative context of this logic space,

---

[15] Bush, 61f.

[16] Aristotle, *Physics*, New translation, introduction and glossary by Joe Sachs, (New Brunswick, NJ: Rutgers University Press, 1995), 243.

[17] Bush, 67.

where valuing reasons constitutes the mind and world relation, comprises the characteristically human ultimate aim. This is the domain of ethics and politics, of applied science and technology, of medical and mechanical knowledge, and much more—all with *eudaimonia* (human happiness) as the ultimate aim. The work of epistemologists is of considerable value in this context, as distinguishing knowledge from mere true belief, including guesswork, is a key to success.

The activity Aristotle identifies with divine happiness, however, is the kind of intelligibility that belongs to the logical space of nature. This includes pure science and metaphysics. Such activity comprises the being-at-work of the intellectual virtues connected to *theōria*. It aims at understanding for its own sake. It is an activity of thought beyond epistemology, beyond evidential structures and reasons. According to Aristotle its ultimate aim is the happiness of the gods.

REFERENCES

Alston, William P. (1983). What's wrong with immediate knowledge? *Synthese* 55, 73-96.

_____. (1986). Internalism and Externalism in Epistemology. *Philosophical Topics* 14: 179-221. Reprinted in Alston 1989.

_____. (1988). The Deontological Conception of Epistemic Justification. *Philosophical Perspectives* 2: 257-299. Reprinted in Alston 1989.

_____. (1989). *Epistemic Justification: Essays in the Theory of Knowledge.* Ithaca: Cornell University Press.

_____. (1991). *Perceiving God: The Epistemology of Religious Experience.* Ithaca: Cornell University Press.

_____. (1993). Epistemic Desiderata. *Philosophy and Phenomenological Research*, 53, 527-551.

_____. (1996). Belief, Acceptance, and Religious Faith. In *Faith, Freedom and Rationality: Philosophy of Religion Today.* Jordan and Howard-Snyder (Eds.). Lanham: Rowman and Littlefield.

_____. (2006). *Beyond Justification: Dimensions of Epistemic Evaluation.* Ithaca: Cornell University Press.

Annas, Julia. (2003) The Structure of Virtue. In *Intellectual Virtue.* DePaul and Zagsebski (Eds.). Oxford: Oxford University Press, 15-33.

_____. (2008) The Phenomenology of Virtue. *Phenomenology and the Cognitive Sciences*, 7, 21-34.

Anscombe, Elizabeth. (1958). Modern Moral Philosophy. *Philosophy*, 33, 1-19.

Aquinas, Thomas. (1947) *Summa Theologica.* English translation by Fathers of English Dominican Province, in three volumes (New York: Benzinger Bros.)

References

Aristotle. (1992). *Nicomachean Ethics*. David Ross (Trans.). New York: Oxford University Press.

_____. (2002) *Nicomachean Ethics*. Joe Sachs (Trans.). Newbury, MA: Focus Publishing.

_____. (1962). *Nicomachean Ethics*. Martin Ostwald (Trans.). Indianapolis: The Bobbs-Merrill Company, Inc.

Battaly, Heather. (2001) Thin Concepts to the Rescue. In *Virtue Epistemology*. A. Fairweather and L. Zagzebski (Eds.). Oxford: Oxford University Press.

_____. (2006). Teaching Intellectual Virtues. In *Teaching Philosophy*, 29:3, 191-222.

Bloomfield, Paul. (2000). Virtue Epistemology and the Epistemology of Virtue. *Philosophy and Phenomenological Research*. LX, No.1, 23-43.

BonJour, Laurence. (1985). *The Structure of Empirical Knowledge*. Cambridge: Harvard University Press.

_____. (2001). Toward a Defense of Empirical Foundationalism. In *Resurrecting Old-Fashioned Foundationalism*. Michael R. DePaul (Ed.). Lanham, MD: Rowman and Littlefield.

Bush, Stephen. (2008). Divine and Human Happiness in Aristotle's Nicomachean Ethics. *Philosophical Review* 117(1), 49-75.

Chisholm, Roderick M. (1980). Justified Belief. *Midwest Studies in Philosophy, vol.5: Studies in Epistemology*, P. French (Ed.). Minneapolis: University of Minneapolis Press.

_____. (1982). Knowledge as Justified True Belief. In *The Foundations of Knowing*. Minneapolis: University of Minneapolis Press, 43-49.

Clarke, Stanley E. and Simpson, Evan (Eds.) (1989). *Anti-Theory in Ethics and Moral Conservatism*. New York: State University of New York Press.

Code, Lorraine. (1987). *Epistemic Responsibility*. Hanover, NH: University Press of New England.

Cohen, Stewart. (1995). Is There an Issue about Justified Belief? *Philosophical Topics*, 23, I, 113-127.

Coleman, Janet. (1995). Machiavelli's *Via Moderna*: Medieval Renaissance Attitudes to History. In *Niccolo Machiavelli's The Prince: New Interdisciplinary Essays*. Manchester: Manchester University Press.

DePaul, Michael and Zagzebski, Linda (Eds.) (2003). *Intellectual Virtue: Perspectives from Ethics and Epistemology*. New York: Oxford University Press.

Driver, Julia. (2001). *Uneasy Virtue*. New York: Cambridge University Press.

Dummett, Michael. (1996). *Frege and Other Philosophers*. Oxford: Oxford University Press.

References 95

Foote, Philippa. (1958). Moral Arguments. *Mind*, 67, 502-513, reprinted in *Virtues and Vices*. Oxford: Blackwell, 1978.

_____. (1959). Moral Beliefs. *Aristotelian Society Proceedings*, 59, 83-104, reprinted in *Virtues and Vices*. Oxford: Blackwell, 1978.

Frege, Gottlob. (1985). *Translations from the Philosophical Writings of Gottlob Frege* (3rd edition). Peter Geach and Max Black (Eds.). Oxford: Basil Blackwell.

_____. (1986). *The Foundations of Arithmetic*. J. L. Austin (Trans.). Evanston, Illinois: Northwestern University Press.

Gettier, Edmund. (1963) Is Justified True Belief Knowledge? *Analysis*, 23, no. 6, 121-123, reprinted in Paul K. Moser and Arnold vander Nat. *Human Knowledge*. 1987. Oxford: Oxford University Press.

Gilligan, Carol. (1982). *In a Different Voice*. Cambridge: Harvard University Press.

Goldman, Alvin. I. (1967). A Causal Theory of Knowing. *Journal of Philosophy* 64.12: 355-372.

_____. (1992). Epistemic Folkways and Scientific Epistemology. In *Liasons: Philosophy Meets the Cognitive and Social Sciences*. Cambridge: MIT Press.

Greco, John. (2000). *Putting Skeptics in Their Place*. New York: Cambridge University Press.

_____. (2004). Virtue Epistemology. In *Stanford Encyclopedia of Philosophy*, http://plato.stanford.edu/entries/epistemology-virtue/.

Harris, C. E. (2002) *Applying Moral Theories*. Belmont, California: Wadsworth Group.

Hempel, Carl. (1950). Problems and Changes in the Empiricist Criterion of Meaning. *Revue Internationale de Philosophie*, 11: 41-63.

Hooker, Brad. (2000). *Ideal Code, Real World*. Oxford: Oxford University Press.

Hookway, Christopher. (2003). How to be a Virtue Epistemologist. In *Intellectual Virtue*. DePaul and Zagzebski (Eds.). Oxford: Oxford University Press.

Hume, David. (1992). *A Treatise of Human Nature* (2nd edition). Text revised and notes by P. H. Nidditch. Oxford: Oxford University Press.

Hursthouse, Rosalind. (2003). Virtue Ethics. In *Stanford Encyclopedia of Philosophy*. http://plato.stanford.edu/entries/ethics-virtue/.

Husserl, Edmund. (1965). Philosophy as Rigorous Science in *Phenomenology and the Crisis of Philosophy*. Quentin Lauer (Trans.). New York: Harper.

References

_____. (1973). *Logical Investigations*. J. N. Findlay (Trans.). London: Routledge.

_____. (1982). *Ideas Pertaining to a Pure Phenomenology and to a Phenomenological Philosophy*. F. Kersten (Trans.). Boston: Martinus Nijhoff.

Jaggar, Alison. (1992). Feminist Ethics. In Lawrence Becker (Ed.), *Encyclopedia of Ethics*. New York: Garland Publishing Co.

James, William. (1904). A World of Pure Experience. *Journal of Philosophy, Psychology, and Scientific Methods,* 1, 533-543, 561-570.

_____. (1907). Pragmatism's Conception of Truth. Lecture 6 in *Pragmatism: A new name for some old ways of thinking*. 1981. New York: Hackett.

_____. (1907) What Pragmatism Means. Lecture 2 in *Pragmatism: A new name for some old ways of thinking*. 1981. New York: Hackett.

Leiter, Brian and Rosen, Michael. (2007). *The Oxford Handbook of Continental Philosophy*. New York: Oxford University Press.

MacIntyre, Alasdair. (1981). *After Virtue*. Notre Dame, Indiana: University of Notre Dame Press.

Matson, Wallace. (2000). *A New History of Philosophy: Volume One: From Thales to Ockham*. Orlando, FL: Harcourt, Inc.

McDowell, John. (1996). *Mind and World*. Cambridge: Harvard University Press.

Montmarquet, James A. (1993). *Epistemic Virtue and Doxastic Responsibility*. Lanham, MD: Rowman and Littlefield.

Moore, George E. (1960). *Principia Ethica*. Cambridge: Cambridge University Press.

Moser, Paul K. and Arnold vander Nat. *Human Knowledge*. 1987. Oxford: Oxford University Press.

Pappas, George S. and Swain, Marshall (Eds.). (1978). *Essays on Knowledge and Justification*. Ithaca: Cornell University Press.

Peters, Francis. (1970). *Greek Philosophical Terms: A Historical Lexicon*. New York: NYU Press.

Plantinga, Alvin. (1993a). *Warrant: The Current Debate*. Oxford: Oxford University Press.

_____. (1993b). *Warrant and Proper Function*. Oxford: Oxford University Press.

_____. (2000). *Warranted Christian Belief*. Oxford: Oxford University Press.

Putnam, Hilary. (1983). Why Reason Can't Be Naturalized. In *Realism and Reason*, Vol. 3 of *Philosophical Papers*. Cambridge: Cambridge University Press, 229-247.

Quine, W. V. (1951) Two Dogmas of Empiricism. *The Philosophical Review 60*: 20–43. Reprinted in his 1953 *From a Logical Point of View* Cambridge: Harvard University Press, and in Paul K. Moser and Arnold vander Nat. *Human Knowledge*. 1987. Oxford: Oxford University Press.

_____. (1969) Epistemology Naturalized. In *Ontological Relativity and Other Essays*. New York: Columbia University Press, 69-90.

Rachels, James. (2003) *The Elements of Moral Philosophy* (4th edition). New York: McGraw-Hill.

Ryle, Gilbert. (1949). *The Concept of Mind*. New York: Barnes and Noble.

Ross, Sir David. (1923). *Aristotle*. London: Methuen and Co. Ltd.

Sachs, Joe. (2002). *Aristotle's Metaphysics*. Translated by Joe Sachs. Santa Fe, NM: Green Lion Press.

_____. (2002). *Nicomachean Ethics*. Translated by Joe Sachs. Newburyport, MA: Focus Publishing, R. Pullins Co.

Sellars, Wilfred. (1956). Empiricism and the Philosophy of Mind. In *Minnesota Studies in the Philosophy of Science* volume 1. Herbert Feigl and Michael Scriven (Eds.). Minneapolis: University of Minnesota Press.

Sider, Theodore. (2001). *Four-Dimensionalism*. Oxford: Oxford University Press.

Slote, Michael. (2001). *Morals from Motives*. Oxford: Oxford University Press.

Sosa, Ernest. (1980). The Raft and the Pyramid: Coherence versus Foundations in the Theory of Knowledge. In *Midwest Studies in Philosophy*, Vol. 5 *Studies in Epistemology*. P. French et. al (Eds.). Minneapolis: University of Minneapolis Press, 3-25, reprinted in Paul K. Moser and Arnold vander Nat. *Human Knowledge*. 1987. Oxford: Oxford University Press, 309-324.

_____. (1991). *Knowledge in Perspective*. New York: Cambridge University Press.

Stocker, Michael. (1976) The Schizophrenia of Modern Ethical Theories. *The Journal of Philosophy*, 73, 453-466.

_____. (1990). *Plural and Conflicting Values*. Oxford: Clarendon Press.

Swain, Marshall. (1972). Knowledge, Causality and Justification. *Journal of Philosophy* 69.11: 291-300.

Williams, Bernard. (1973) *Utilitarianism: For and Against*. New York: Cambridge University Press.

_____. (1973). Morality and the Emotions. *Problems of the Self*. New York: Cambridge University Press.

References

_____. (1981). Persons, Character, and Morality. *Moral Luck*. New York: Cambridge University Press.

_____. (1981). Moral Luck. *Moral Luck*. New York: Cambridge University Press.

_____. (1981). Utilitarianism and Moral Self-Indulgence. *Moral Luck*. New York: Cambridge University Press.

_____. (1985). *Ethics and the Limits of Philosophy*. Cambridge: Harvard University Press.

Young, Charles. (1988). Aristotle on Temperance. *The Philosophical Review* Vol. XCVII, No. 4: 521-542.

Zagzebski, Linda Trinkaus. (1996). *Virtues of the Mind: An Inquiry into the Nature of Virtue and the Ethical Foundations of Knowledge*. New York: Cambridge University Press.

_____. (2000). Précis of Virtues of the Mind. *Philosophy and Phenomenological Research*, 60, 169-177.

INDEX

analytic philosophy, 1-2, 7-9, 14, 42, 47, 51-59, 80-81
boorishness, 34
breath hold, 31
buffoonery, 34
cantankerousness, 34
coherentism, 64,-66, 68, 70-72
conceptual analysis, 2, 50-60, 68, 73
continental philosophy, 47, 49-50, 53
deontology, 1, 9, 11, 15, 18, 22
dissipation, 33
epistemic desiderata, 2, 68-70, 81, 83
epistemic justification, 2, 60-61, 64-68, 70, 81, 85,
epistemic normativity, 69-73
ergon, 90
ēthikē aretē, 2, 22-30
ēthos, 5-6, 30-31
ethos, 30-31
eudaimonia, 33, 35, 86, 89-92
externalism, 67-68, 73
fact/value gap (logical gap), 37, 39, 43, 47
friendliness, 34
foundationalism, 64-66, 68, 70-72, 81
gravitational force, 24, 46, 84-85
hexis, 26, 29-32
intellectual virtue(s), 2, 61, 70-78, 81
internalism, 67-69, 72, 74

(JTB) model of knowledge, 61-64
Learner's Paradox (Paradox of Analysis), 51-52
logical empiricism (logical positivism), 43, 53-54, 57-59, 81
makarios, 90-91
maximum condition, virtues are a, 31
natural law, 40-42
obsequiousness, 34
phenomenology, 32, 47-51, 53, 67
philosophy of mathematics, 47-53
phronesis, 15, 86-87, 90
psychē, 26-29
self-control, 32-33
teleology, 43-47
temperance, 32-33
ultimate aims, 86, 89-92
up to us, virtues and vices are, 34-35, 86-87
utilitarianism, 1, 10-15, 17-22
verificationism, 54-57
virtue-reliabilism, 74-75
virtue-responsibilism, 74-78
virtus, 22, 24-26